PUBLIC SCHOOL CHOICE
VS.
PRIVATE SCHOOL VOUCHERS

Public School Choice vs. Private School Vouchers

Richard D. Kahlenberg, *Editor*

A Century Foundation Volume of Essays

The Century Foundation Press * New York

The Century Foundation sponsors and supervises timely analyses of economic policy, foreign affairs, and domestic political issues. Not-for-profit and nonpartisan, it was founded in 1919 and endowed by Edward A. Filene.

Library of Congress Cataloging-in-Publication Data

Public school choice vs. private school vouchers / Richard D. Kahlenberg, ed.
p. cm.
ISBN 0-87078-484-6 (pbk. : alk. paper)
1. School choice--United States. 2. Educational vouchers--United States. I. Kahlenberg, Richard D. II. Title.
LB1027.9.P73 2003
379.1'11'0973--dc21

2003006438

Cover design and illustration by Claude Goodwin.
Manufactured in the United States of America.

Foreword

During the past several decades, the triumph of capitalism's central ideas has been remarkable. Free markets, by most measures, seem to have overwhelmingly won the competition with alternative forms of economic organization. Perhaps it is not surprising, then, that the structures that have worked so well in the private sector, increasingly, have come to be viewed as solutions to public sector missions. Today, this belief in "privatization" extends well beyond the obvious case for selling off state-run businesses to encompass the process of moving basic services out of government control and into the hands of private vendors.

The attractiveness of this approach has fueled a profound shift in the United States and much of the world. Even the most traditional of public services—fire departments and emergency medical services—in many communities have been placed in the hands of private corporations. Despite some glaring failures such as privatized airport security systems, the embarrassments caused by several privatized state prisons, and other mixed results from attempts to shift public services to the private marketplace, powerful political forces continue to press for further privatization of almost all public enterprises, from Social Security to Amtrak to our public libraries.

Emboldened by a recent U.S. Supreme Court decision permitting the use of public funds for religious schools, private school advocates now are placing renewed emphasis on plans to promote school vouchers throughout the nation. Supporters argue that the magic of the private marketplace will improve our education system, particularly by liberating low-income and minority students from failing public schools. Advocates argue that privatization also will lead to more variety, greater than that provided by the fifteen thousand local school districts in the United States. Those who support privatization contend that widely different school experiences can better match the interests, needs, and strengths of individual students and teachers.

But if markets do deliver almost unlimited variety, it is fair to ask if this is really what we are after in our publicly funded education system. Public education was introduced not only to provide a skilled workforce but also to meet the needs of our diverse democracy. Would public subsidies to religious academies, to schools that teach ethnic hatred, or to schools that teach "science" that comes from holy texts lead to a more tolerant and engaged citizenry? If a central goal of public education is to prepare the next generation for participation in America's experiment in multicultural democracy, do we want to subsidize parents who choose schools that reflect narrow perspectives on basic questions?

Like many supporters of privatization, advocates of vouchers often take it for granted that the market delivers better results than the public sector. In fact, there is little evidence that performance in voucher programs differs significantly from performance in public schools, when similar students are compared. What is more, there is almost no evidence comparing the performance of students in voucher programs to those in school choice programs within the public school system.

Many of the areas of contention concerning school privatization need more independent study. But already there are serious studies available addressing some of the central questions on policy in this area. What are, for example, the obvious and not so obvious costs of a private educational marketplace? Can diverse educational offerings be obtained by affording greater choice within the public school system? Can the achievement gains (sometimes) associated with vouchers be attributed to something inherent in private schooling, or is it mostly a function of the more affluent and self-selected mix of students and parents found in private schools?

Over the past four years, The Century Foundation has supported papers, articles, books, events, and a task force to examine these questions. These projects include Gordon MacInnes's white paper, "Kids Who Pick the Wrong Parents and Other Victims of Voucher Schemes"; a National Press Club event on "Progressive Alternatives to School Vouchers," featuring Brent Staples, Adam Urbanski, Christopher Edley, and Elliot Mincberg; *A Notion at Risk: Preserving Public Education as an Engine for Social Mobility*, which includes a chapter on charter schools by Amy Stuart Wells and colleagues; Richard D. Kahlenberg's *All Together Now: Creating Middle-Class Schools through Public School Choice*;

and the Report of The Century Foundation Task Force on the Common School, chaired by Lowell Weicker, *Divided We Fail: Coming Together through Public School Choice*. This collection of readings was prepared because we thought it would be helpful to assemble relevant excerpts from these projects in a single place. In addition, it includes new selections written by Century Foundation staff and fellows Thad Hall, Ruy Teixeira, and Bernard Wasow, as well as insightful articles by friends of the Foundation, including Helen Ladd, Edward Fiske, Sean Reardon, John Yun, and Richard Just.

These research efforts find, on the whole, that private school vouchers are not a panacea for what ails education in the United States. Taken together, the studies indicate that there are significant issues of accountability, capacity, segregation, and stratification in privatized initiatives. While those who are pushing private school vouchers have taken to referring to public schools by the vaguely authoritarian-sounding name "government-run schools," the consensus among the authors in this volume is that having the public elect officials who will help shape the values and principles our children are taught is essential in a democratic society. Likewise, while voucher advocates complain of an inefficient public education "monopoly," these authors find that a system of choice can flourish within our nation's thousands of public school districts and nearly one hundred thousand individual public schools. The volume shows that the advantages private schools appear to offer are most likely a function of the student and parental mix that comes from institutions selecting their populations, and that public school choice can harness these positive characteristics to benefit all students, not just a few.

In short, this volume seeks to go beyond the empty arguments about whether we should deliver all our social challenges to the magic of the marketplace. It aims to call the bluff of voucher supporters: if we are all truly concerned about schools that give low-income students better opportunities and provide a variety of school offerings, why not greatly expand choice within the existing system of public education, where everyone plays by the same set of rules and all schools are publicly accountable? We hope that this volume sheds light on that more fruitful path. On behalf our Trustees, I thank the collection's editor, Richard Kahlenberg, and all the contributors for their efforts.

Richard C. Leone, *President*
The Century Foundation
July 2003

Contents

1.

Introduction

The Three Liberal Responses to Private School Vouchers

Richard D. Kahlenberg

There is a strange tenor to the debate over school vouchers, with conservative groups, not known for a history of commitment to the downtrodden, evincing a newfound moral passion for liberating poor children from bad schools. They note that the wealthy can choose high-quality schools, by purchasing a home in an area with top-ranked public schools or by paying tuition to a good private school, and argue that poor families should have the same right.[1] This sentiment represents an enormous shift from the days of racial desegregation, when conservatives championed the "neighborhood" school above all other values. Now conservatives point out that the neighborhood school is not such a great deal for children stuck in poor neighborhoods and argue, with great egalitarian passion, that everyone should have the right to choose a good school. There are at least three possible responses.

One response is to join conservatives. The new emphasis on equity has convinced some liberals that conservatives are right: vouchers are the way to go. Well-respected liberal thinkers like Joseph Califano, Andrew Young, Robert Reich, Matthew Miller, Arthur Levine, William Raspberry, Martha Minow, and the editorial page editors of the *Washington Post* have all come around to thinking that vouchers are worth a try.[2] Polls find, likewise, that young African Americans support vouchers by more than two to one.[3] A failure to sign on to vouchers is seen by many of these liberal proponents as a simple matter of interest group politics: powerful teachers unions will not let Democrats do what is right for poor kids.

A second response is to charge conservatives with hypocrisy and continue to plug away at ongoing public school reform. Advocates point out that conservatives are not serious when they say throw open the doors to everyone; certainly they do not mean that the poor have a right to an equal representation at St. Albans or Andover. Instead, this group dismisses the new conservative rhetoric about liberating poor kids as insincere and pushes for ways to improve neighborhood public schools through traditional approaches like reducing class size, increasing teacher pay, and the like. The leadership of the National Education Association, for example, says Americans "want quality public education in their neighborhood school, and that's what we should be working toward."[4]

There is a third possible response, which sees the conservative argument in support of vouchers as an enormous opportunity. While vouchers themselves are wrongheaded, this group asks, what sort of public policy response could be crafted to build on the wholly legitimate premise of voucher advocates that it is immoral to trap poor children in failing schools? This volume lays out that alternative path, recognizing that the ongoing efforts to fix economically segregated neighborhood schools are unlikely to succeed and that private school vouchers are likely to make things even worse. Though not every contributor would necessarily agree, the core thesis of the volume as a whole is that public school choice, properly structured, can garner all the benefits of vouchers (allowing poor kids to escape bad schools, providing more variety in schooling, and shaking up the bureaucracy with competitive pressures) while avoiding the many pitfalls (increased racial and economic segregation, weakened social cohesion, reduced achievement for those left behind, and greater reliance on unaccountable institutions). Whereas many school reformers have rhetorically embraced "public school choice" as a crisp and convenient rebuttal to the argument for school vouchers, this volume suggests that public school choice must be at the very center of school reform efforts.

Over the past few years, The Century Foundation has committed a fair amount of time to developing the dialogue on school vouchers and public school reform, and we thought it would be useful to assemble these materials in a single place. This volume also contains a number of essays written specifically for this collection as well as previously published articles written by friends of the Foundation.

Part I of the volume exposes the false promise of school vouchers. Gordon MacInnes's essay reveals the claims of voucher proponents to be overblown and raises a number of probing questions: What is the capacity of the private school sector, which now serves only 10 percent of American schoolchildren, to absorb more students? If new schools emerge in response to demand, are they likely to be of the low caliber seen in proprietary trade schools that arose to take advantage of government funds made available through higher education vouchers? Will private schools, which pride themselves on independence, be willing to subject themselves to accountability schemes? Richard Leone's essay outlines the unfairness of the sister proposal for private school tax exemptions, which provide the bulk of the benefits to those least in need of extra help—the wealthy. The volume then proceeds to challenge four central myths that have grown up around the voucher debate.

Myth number 1 is that vouchers raise student achievement, both for students who receive vouchers and for those who remain in public schools and see their schools transformed by competition. Gordon MacInnes looks at the early research on vouchers, which on the whole shows no significant positive effects from private schooling once differences in background are considered and finds no substantial gains from the nation's first voucher program in Milwaukee. Bernard Wasow then analyzes the data in the most recent studies and concludes that the case for vouchers is unconvincing. The achievement results are mixed for voucher recipients not only in Milwaukee but also in privately funded programs in Washington, Dayton, and New York. Those who remain in public schools may benefit from the competition of choice, but those benefits also accrue to public school choice, he notes. Finally, Richard Kahlenberg finds that any apparent achievement gains for students receiving vouchers are most likely to disappear when small voucher programs are scaled up. Even if the claims of voucher advocates are taken at face value—that African American students from low-income families benefit from existing voucher experiments—the benefits may disappear once large numbers of poor children are given access to private schools. The current advantages those students enjoy in voucher schools—having particularly motivated and well-behaved classmates and actively engaged parents—will quickly fade away once programs are expanded and voucher schools come to resemble high-poverty public schools.

Myth number 2 is that vouchers are part of a new civil rights movement. The notion is trumpeted by the ubiquitous ads of the Black Alliance for Educational Options (BAEO) and by conservative politicians not otherwise known as champions of civil rights. As Richard Leone points out in a brief essay, President Bush's comparison of the recent Supreme Court voucher decision to *Brown v. Board of Education* is nothing short of astonishing given the history of school vouchers and their likely effects in the future. An excerpt from The Century Foundation's Task Force on the Common School (chaired by Lowell P. Weicker, Jr.) outlines why the experience in other countries—Sweden, Chile, and the Netherlands—indicates that vouchers will likely lead to further segregation and hurt poor and minority students left behind. Edward B. Fiske and Helen F. Ladd's article demonstrates how unregulated school choice in New Zealand led to precisely that result. Sean F. Reardon and John T. Yun's piece finds that while American public schools are hardly models of integration, private schools are even more segregated. Amy Stuart Wells and colleagues provide an additional reason to be skeptical: charter schools often further segregate students. Their evidence raises concerns that voucher proposals, which often allow schools to decide whom to admit, are likely to fare even worse on this score. Gordon MacInnes provides still more evidence that unregulated choice (public or private) can often mean segregation.

Myth number 3 is that vouchers are good for democracy because they nourish religious and nongovernmental institutions, which, in turn, encourage civic engagement. Essays by Richard Kahlenberg, Richard Just, and Gordon MacInnes question whether democratic unity is really well served by a system that uses public funds to support private schools that may appeal explicitly to particular ethnic groups or that harden religious differences. The private sector operates best by finding ways to segment markets and, as the late Albert Shanker, head of the American Federation of Teachers, noted, under voucher programs "you'll end up with kids of different religions, nationalities and languages going off to different schools to maintain their separateness and I think we'd have a terrible social price to pay for it."[5] Justice David Souter's dissent in the 2002 U.S. Supreme Court's decision in *Zelman v. Simmons-Harris* upholding Cleveland's voucher program notes that every religion teaches that other religions are in error, which is their right. But in a country as diverse as ours, public funds need to be used to emphasize common ideas and allegiance to country, not to support teaching that will help tear at the social fabric. As Just writes, "The inane logic of vouchers would leave us with a stark choice: either become a country that pays religious institutions to proselytize to children of other faiths, or become a country that educates children of different religions separately." While the *Zelman* case settled the constitutional questions about vouchers, the serious policy objections regarding aid for religious indoctrination of young children in a multicultural democracy remain to be answered.

Myth number 4 is that the American public is clamoring for vouchers. Ruy Teixeira remarks that in fact the public generally likes public schools. Despite the expenditure of hundreds of millions of dollars by conservatives on voucher programs, less than one-tenth of 1 percent of American students use publicly funded vouchers. To the extent Americans support vouchers, it may be fairly interpreted as a plea to do something dramatic rather than as an endorsement of privatization per se. Thad Hall's essay notes that Congress has little appetite for school vouchers. Few bills are introduced as even symbolic gestures, and, despite control of the House, the Republican leadership has not generally pushed for votes on vouchers as they have on other conservative priorities. Indeed, President George W. Bush's signature No Child Left Behind Act provides for greater public school choice rather than vouchers. Voucher proposals largely have been limited to the District of Columbia, which has no genuine voice in Congress.

While school vouchers are bad public policy on the whole, it is incumbent on opponents to articulate a principled and realistic alternative that will respond to the legitimate premise of voucher proponents: that compulsory assignment of students to high-poverty schools is unfair and immoral, given the grave odds of failing that students in those schools face. Part II of the book articulates the affirmative case for public school choice.

The overview of this section begins with excerpts from a discussion The Century Foundation sponsored assembling representatives of the three communities most opposed to vouchers—civil rights advocates (Christopher Edley, Jr.), members of teachers unions (Adam Urbanski), and civil libertarians (Elliot Mincberg)—and giving them the opportunity to speak about what they favor as progressive alternatives to vouchers. The overview also includes a *Washington Post* op-ed by Richard Kahlenberg on public school choice.

The volume then goes on to lay out the considerable evidence that public school choice, if structured properly, will raise student achievement, promote equity in education, and better prepare students to be citizens in a democracy—the very goals voucher proponents identify. Richard Kahlenberg's essay discusses how "controlled public school choice"—employed in Cambridge, Massachusetts; Montclair, New Jersey; and elsewhere—gives every family the right to choose among a variety of public schools within a given geographic zone. Parents are polled to find out what sorts of schools they would like for their children, and then every single school becomes a magnet school, with something special to offer—from a "Core Knowledge" curriculum to a Montessori teaching approach, from a music and arts theme to an emphasis on computers. Families rank preferences, and school administrators honor those choices with an eye to ensuring that all schools have a healthy socioeconomic or racial mix. Requiring all families to participate in the choice process avoids the problem experienced by many private and public school choice programs in which only the most motivated families choose to participate and the least engaged are left behind.

Why is it important that the choice program contain fairness guidelines to ensure that choice promotes economic integration? The Report of The Century Foundation Task Force on the Common School, excerpted in this volume, concludes that "of all the various strategies available, research suggests that the best method for improving education in the United States is to eliminate the harmful effects of concentrated school poverty." High-poverty schools are marked by diminished expectations, low-quality teaching, minimal parental involvement, inadequate resources, and high levels of disorder. By contrast, schools in middle-class areas tend to work fairly well, and all students, whether from low-income or middle-class backgrounds, have been found to perform at much higher levels when they attend such schools than when they attend high-poverty schools. Public school choice is therefore essential to raising achievement because it provides the most practical way to prevent economically segregated neighborhoods from producing economically segregated schools.

The report also includes a summary of two case studies. The first focuses on Cambridge, where the schools are economically integrated and 90 percent of parents receive one of their top three choices. The second examines St. Louis, where thousands of urban students attend suburban schools and enjoy much higher levels of success than those attending segregated schools with extra funding. Voucher supporters have made much of the fact that under the Cleveland voucher program not a single suburban public school chose to receive city students with vouchers because to them this is evidence that private schools must be included, but St. Louis's example suggests the proper financial incentives can garner active suburban participation.[6]

Finally, Richard Kahlenberg's review of Terry Moe's book on public opinion and vouchers notes that even such ardent voucher advocates as Moe must concede that support for public school choice outstrips support for private school vouchers. Simply put, people like choice, and they like public schools, so they naturally gravitate to plans that combine elements of both. The number of students using public school choice within existing school district boundaries stands at 5 million. Another 300,000 students cross school district lines in public school choice programs. And the number of students in districts with economic school integration plans (some using public school choice, others accomplishing integration by redrawing neighborhood school boundaries) has skyrocketed from 20,000 in 1999 to more than 400,000 today. By contrast, about 14,000 students currently participate in publicly funded private school voucher programs.

Despite these numbers, in the public dialogue voucher supporters have enjoyed what they might call a rhetorical "monopoly" on the issue of choice. They have been able to point to the grave inequities in education to say, "it's unfair to trap poor kids in bad schools," and so long as the response was a call for gradual reform of urban public education, voucher advocates held the upper hand. But the public school choice alternative takes away the best arguments for vouchers and provides a solution more congenial to the American people—a system of choice that is fair to all, that will serve very large numbers of students, and that simultaneously honors America's historic commitment to public education.

Liberating poor children from bad schools is at bottom a moral imperative. More choice is coming because the public demands it, so the issue is not choice versus no choice but what kind of choice. Should we pour public funds into the 10 percent of schools (private institutions) that provide exclusive education, that promote particular religious beliefs, and that are beyond democratic control, or into the 90 percent of schools that take all comers, help bind together people of diverse races and religions, and are accountable to the public through their elected leaders? As the evidence in this volume demonstrates, the right choice is clear.

Part I. The False Promise of School Vouchers

This part of the book outlines why school vouchers are unlikely to deliver on a host of promises. The authors raise serious questions about capacity, quality, and accountability and go on to challenge four central myths propogated by voucher supporters. The essays contend that in practice vouchers will not raise student achievement, are hardly part of a new civil rights movement to liberate disadvantaged minority students, will not invigorate our democracy and civil society, and do not command the support of the American public.

2.

Overview

Overblown Claims and Nagging Questions

Gordon MacInnes

What's Good for Chelsea . . .

When then President-elect Bill Clinton and his wife Hillary announced in January 1993 that their daughter, Chelsea, would attend Sidwell Friends School, a selective and expensive private school, their decision was immediately criticized. The *New York Times*, an opponent of vouchers, opined that Mr. Clinton had "a larger obligation [than that of parent] that he took on by campaigning as an advocate of public education. He has not served the spirit of that obligation by choosing a private school."[1]

Proponents of vouchers, on the other hand, attacked the Clintons as hypocrites. Typical was the reaction of Clint Bolick of the Institute for Justice, which provides legal representation to voucher advocates: "Bill Clinton, the self-described advocate of public schools, finds that not a single public school in D.C. is adequate for his daughter," Mr. Bolick said, *"and we'd like to see other parents, particularly low-income parents, have the same choice as Bill Clinton."*[2]

Excerpts from Gordon MacInnes, "Kids Who Pick the Wrong Parents and Other Victims of Voucher Schemes," The Century Foundation, New York, 1999.

The enthusiasm of prominent conservatives for wanting to help the poorest children in the nation's capital attend its most prestigious schools deserves emphasis and analysis. Consider: the tuition and fees for Sidwell in 1998 were around $15,500; the District of Columbia spends about $9,000 for each of its eighty thousand students. Extending the same choice that was made by the Clintons to every D.C. student would require taxpayers to finance the difference between Sidwell's costs and those of the public schools, theoretically an additional $520 million or so. This figure does not include the cost of paying for the tuition of the D.C. residents already enrolled in private and parochial schools (an additional sixteen thousand students). Of course, most D.C. parents would not try to get their children into schools as costly as Sidwell (or any private school, for that matter). But even if only a few parents take Mr. Bolick's promise to heart, their experience is most likely to be frustrating, if not heartbreaking. The more who try, the greater the agony.

Sidwell is selective, very selective. Fewer than 1,100 students are enrolled in its fourteen grades, pre-kindergarten through grade 12, with about 450 in its high school. Its 1998 ninth-grade class of 117 was made up mostly of Sidwell middle school graduates, but 24 came from other schools. Sidwell accepted only 19 percent of the 176 students who applied for those 24 places, a rejection rate mirroring that of all but the most selective Ivy League universities. So, just how likely is it that Sidwell would show any interest in students hoping to transfer from the District's public schools, even assuming that taxpayers would pay all their costs via Mr. Bolick's voucher?

To start, no student with a disability requiring special assistance need apply—Sidwell has no program to help with such problems. This would eliminate about 10 percent of the District's students, who are classified as handicapped. Nor should any immigrant student still shaky in English expect consideration—Sidwell looks for those who have mastered English, not those who are struggling with it.

The prospects for the balance of the District's eighty thousand students are not much better. Sidwell does not offer formal remedial instruction. Assuming that it would at least consider students who tested as "advanced" on standardized written exams, 99 percent of the District's students would be ineligible (D.C. eighth graders were dead last among students from forty-five states who took the National Assessment of Educational Progress [NAEP] exam in 1996—and by a lot).[3] If money were no object, how many of the District's vouchered students might find themselves on Sidwell's parklike campus? Two or three, maybe. What is more likely, however, is that Sidwell and comparable schools would simply decline to participate at all. Make that number zero.

Mr. Bolick might back off by saying that he was really thinking of the other independent and religious private schools in the District. Washington has dozens of religious schools, plus eleven other schools like Sidwell, that are listed in guides to private schools. This latter group enrolls a total of 5,409 students in pre-kindergarten through grade 12, at tuitions that range from $6,650 to $15,070 (plus miscellaneous fees and travel, of course). In 1998, these schools accepted a total of 663 students into their ninth-grade classes (the traditional transfer year for high school), but 412 of those were admitted to just two of the less-selective schools.[4]

One must quickly conclude that Mr. Bolick is not serious about a voucher program premised on giving poor, minority parents in dangerous neighborhoods a realistic choice to send their children to their city's most prestigious schools (most such schools are already energetic in searching out able, poor, minority students). The holes in his position raise questions:

- If voucher proponents do not have schools like Sidwell in mind, what kinds of schools will parents be able to select?
- What is the capacity of nonpublic schools to absorb students who want to get out of failed school districts?
- What is the likelihood that parents will want to move their kids to a new school if vouchers are available? What is the profile of those who use vouchers and those who do not?
- If parents choose nonpublic schools, how likely is it that their child will be better educated?
- If existing schools are quickly filled because of vouchers, what kind of schools will be created to meet the unfilled demand?
- What choices will handicapped students have? What of those who are deficient in English?

- What about public school students whose parents pay no effective attention to their children's schooling?
- Will American voters accept the mixing of public dollars with religious indoctrination that is required if vouchers are to reach many students?

Those who oppose vouchers face an uncomfortable question of their own. Is it fair to deny educational opportunities to low-income children with motivated parents in order to maintain a "better mix" of strivers and nonstrivers in public schools?

These are some of the questions we will seek to answer.

Stories Conservatives Like to Tell

Advocates tell stories. Stories deflect the demand for precision and documentation. They make an argument more human, more readable, more persuasive.

Here are two composite stories that voucher enthusiasts like to tell.

> Rhonda Perkins lives in a poor, Detroit neighborhood with her ten-year-old daughter, Tamika. Rhonda, a former welfare recipient, is a convenience store clerk; Tamika attends the neighborhood public school. Rhonda works with Tamika every night on her homework—no television is permitted between 6 and 8 P.M. Because Rhonda believes that Tamika is assigned too little homework and given too few writing projects, she makes an appointment with her fourth-grade teacher to lobby for more (which means losing a half-day of work).
>
> Arriving at the graffiti-scarred school entrance, Rhonda is subjected to a metal detector search and directed to the main office, where she is coolly received. After waiting twenty minutes, she is led to the teacher conference room, a dirty, shabby room that doubles as a staff lounge. Tamika's teacher, Mrs. Green, has taught just three years, hired after she lost her job as a claims adjuster. After hearing Rhonda's questions and suggestions, Mrs. Green informs her that the current level of homework is within the guidelines set by Detroit's Elementary Instructional Division, that it is considered "age appropriate," that extra reading assignments cannot be given because the school library has too few volumes, and, besides, the

> teacher has her hands full with twenty-five energetic fourth graders plus burdensome paperwork for the folks "downtown." As to additional writing exercises, Mrs. Green cannot work with Tamika without exceeding the "home preparation" time in the teachers' contract or threatening the self-esteem of Tamika's classmates who are not interested in additional writing projects.

Tough luck, Ms. Perkins. Your daughter's education is in the hands of a suffocating bureaucracy, uninspired leadership, and a teachers' union that protects incompetents and worse.

Contrast Rhonda's tale of indifference and patronizing treatment with this experience:

> Carmen Martinez lives in Milwaukee. After battling unsuccessfully to get her daughter, Julia, transferred to the gifted and talented program, Carmen called the Parent Information Center to request information on conveniently located schools that emphasize strong academics and mastery of basic skills. She soon received six colorful and clearly written brochures from one Lutheran, one independent, and four Catholic schools. Narrowing her choice to three, Carmen took time off from her job as a bilingual receptionist to visit the schools and to talk to the teachers Julia would have if enrolled. Everyone was hospitable and encouraging. The teachers reviewed the curriculum and asked a lot of questions about Julia's interests, status, and weaknesses.
>
> Carmen selected Resurrection Catholic Academy because she liked the emphasis on discipline and religious instruction on top of a more demanding academic schedule. And it was safe. The Milwaukee Parental Choice Program paid Resurrection $4,894 to take Julia for the year; the Milwaukee public schools arranged Julia's busing. All Carmen had to do was to pay an extra $45 a month so that Julia could take advantage of the after-school program. Now Julia is flourishing and happy and Carmen is active in the home/school association.

The proponents of "parental choice" and school vouchers make it sound so easy, don't they? After all, who could know better the educational needs of children than their parents? And what could be more American than to give parents the right to decide the character and emphasis of their child's schooling?

There are other stories that are just as telling and important, but are never included in the voucher storybook.

Stories Voucher Advocates Won't Tell

> Patrice Taylor, age twenty-six, lives in a squalid public housing project on Chicago's South Side. Having had her first child at age sixteen, she never went beyond the tenth grade. Her second child followed two years later (by a different father), and she now has a two-year-old by a third man. Her ten- and eight-year-olds attend the local school.
>
> Patrice is tired of being a mother. She supplements her meager welfare allotment by reselling some of the drugs that she buys for her own use and engaging in occasional prostitution. She frequently leaves her ten-year-old daughter in charge at night so that she can "keep in touch with her friends," despite official warnings that she could lose her children for endangering their welfare.
>
> When asked, Patrice agrees that "education is very important" and that it is the "key to a better life for my kids." Yet when her son's teacher sends a note home requesting a conference about Rayton's "acting out" and "uncooperative behavior," Patrice pays no attention. When the CEO Foundation mails her an announcement of an "opportunity scholarship" for her kids to attend the local parochial school, Patrice doesn't even open the letter.

Too bad, kids, you picked the wrong parents. Here is a second kind of story that the voucher lobby doesn't tell:

> Will and Wendy Chapman, both in their mid-thirties, live on Philadelphia's Main Line. He is a stockbroker, she is a partner in a big, downtown law firm. Their annual income exceeds $400,000. Both Ivy League graduates, they have assiduously planned the education of their two children. Each started at a preschool program at age four that conducted interviews and oral tests before admission. They then graduated to selective same-sex schools. The tuition for one third-grade girl and one fifth-grade boy totals $28,000 a year.
>
> When Pennsylvania enacted a universal voucher program that guaranteed every family a tax credit equaling the per-student average expenditure in the local public school ($9,250), the Chapmans signed up. Who can blame them?

Do Vouchers Improve Education for Poor City Children?

Voucher proponents hammer the theme of public school failure in cities. Statistics and anecdotes pile up to portray the dead certainty that public schools cannot work because they are too bureaucratized, too unionized, and too stifling. The answer seems clear and obvious: parental choice in general, vouchers specifically. But although voucher advocates promise to please parents like Rhonda and Carmen, they have nothing to say to those like Patrice. We have no way of knowing how many Patrices there are in urban America, but we can lay out the dimensions of the problem facing voucher advocates (and anyone else who cares about educational opportunity and equity).

Liberals and conservatives agree that the most intractable problem of educational performance is to be found in the nation's older cities. With just short of 30 percent of the nation's population, the central cities are home to 45 percent of the poor, almost half of poor children under age eighteen, and a near majority of welfare families. The magnitudes are important to keep in mind: of the more than 50 million U.S. schoolchildren, about 9.5 million live below the poverty line—and half of them live in central cities. The cities bear a disproportionate burden in educating children of immigrants, many of whom arrive without competency in English and, increasingly, without schooling in their native tongue. Fast-growing, large city districts are typically found in the states that absorb most immigrants: California, New York, Florida, Texas, New Jersey, and Illinois. Adding to the cities' problems is their responsibility to students who are classified as disabled under federal law, who average 12 percent of all students nationally.

Without poor city kids, there is no compelling case to be made for vouchers. To be sure, public schools everywhere could be better, more academically oriented, and more effective in treating students with respect. But most middle-class families are satisfied with their children's educational options, and the wealthy have already chosen private schools. So far, voucher advocates and the schools that take voucher students have been unresponsive to the needs of, and silent about the opportunities for, Patrice's children and for disabled and non-English-speaking students. The voucher movement rides on the back of poor, minority city children, and it is fair to expect the movement to account for its performance. These approximately 5 million kids will be the focus of our analysis.

Vouchers for Everyone!

The voucher movement traces its ideological roots to two theoretical works. Milton Friedman first advanced the idea of vouchers in 1955 and elaborated on it in his popular 1962 book, *Freedom and Capitalism*, as an alternative to his first choice, fully private education. In Friedman's ideal world there would be no public schools and no tax funding of elementary and secondary education. Instead, each family would be fully responsible for financing its own children's education (although low-income families would be able to obtain public subsidies).

Friedman sees ancillary benefits to his proposal: "imposing the costs on the parents would tend to equalize the social and private costs of having children and so promote a *better* distribution of families by size."[5] Although Friedman's goal of smaller poor families might be frustrated by his willingness to subsidize their educational costs, he is certain that society would benefit if poor Americans had fewer children.

Conceding that there is little chance of eliminating government's role in financing education, Friedman's fallback position is universal vouchers. He sees no reason why government should both finance and operate schools. In Friedman's vision, public schools are replaced by nonprofit, independent schools or profit-making corporations. "The role of government," Friedman wrote, "would be limited to insuring that the schools met certain minimum standards, such as the inclusion of minimum common content in their programs, much as it now inspects restaurants to insure . . . minimum sanitary standards."[6]

Friedman argues that vouchers would be likely to result in "smaller governmental expenditures on schooling, yet higher total expenditures." How? "[Vouchers] would enable parents to buy what they want more efficiently and thereby lead them to spend more than they now do directly and indirectly through taxation."[7] Friedman assumes that most parents are interested in a solid academic education for their children and not the extraneous activities like "basket weaving, social dancing," and "coaches and corridors." Vouchers would spur competition, introduce a market standard for teacher salaries, and stimulate much greater variety in schools. And since public schools serve segregated neighborhoods, Friedman notes, vouchers would actually reduce stratification by race and economic class.

The second work, *Politics, Markets, and America's Schools* by John Chubb and Terry Moe, was published by the Brookings Institution in 1990. The book attracted extensive commentary, in part because its publisher was described as a major "liberal" think tank, and that fact was magnified to assert substantial erosion in support for public education among its traditional allies. Whereas Friedman relied on economic theory to reach his conclusions and policy prescriptions, Chubb and Moe arrive at the same conclusions by analyzing the nature of democratic institutions. They go further than Friedman by asserting that high-performing schools are not just unlikely—they are inconsistent with the operations of representative democracy.

The key to understanding why America's public schools are failing is to be found in a deeper understanding of how its traditional institutions of democratic control actually work. The nation is experiencing a crisis in public education not because these democratic institutions have functioned perversely or improperly or unwisely but because they have functioned quite normally. Democratic control normally produces ineffective schools.[8] This is how it works.

The Chubb-Moe thesis lays waste to the hope of friendly critics that public schools can be reformed and made more effective. Why? Because not everyone wants schools focused narrowly on academic achievement—and in a responsive system those who want cheerleaders, auto mechanics, and drug prevention education are able to get their way, too. So confident are they of their institutional analysis that Chubb and Moe pronounce the choice system to be the exclusive solution to the nation's educational ills:

> Without being too literal about it, we think reformers would do well to entertain the notion that choice is a panacea. This is our way of saying that choice is not like the other reforms and should not be combined with them as a part of a reformist strategy for improving America's public schools. . . . [Choice] has the capacity all by itself to bring about the kind of transformation that, for years, reformers have been seeking to engineer in myriad other ways.[9]

The heart of the Chubb-Moe thesis rests on a dubious statistical argument that leads to the claim that *school organization* variables contribute more to explaining student achievement gains in high school than do student achievement as measured in tenth grade, or the social and economic status of the students' parents, or the socioeconomic makeup of the school. This alleged finding turns James S. Coleman's *Equality of Educational Opportunity* report on its head.[10] Not surprisingly, Chubb and Moe find that private schools are much more likely to exhibit the organizational characteristics they've identified as positive (for example, principal's leadership, teacher collegiality, absence of bureaucratic controls, and so on) than are public schools.

Let's be clear: the fathers of market-based solutions are not to be satisfied with incremental or piecemeal victories such as interdistrict public school choice or charter schools. They seek nothing less than the dismantling of public education and its replacement with a system of tax financing that allows parents to direct all school spending and, in the process, eliminates the notion of the common school. And their political allies are just as ideological, if more flexible.

Until universal vouchers prevail, conservative activists will happily ally themselves with those public school advocates who support charter schools, for example, as a way to energize public schools and deflect the pressure for vouchers. Such alliances are strictly tactical and temporary. One voucher advocate noted: "Extending school choice to include private, independent schools is a major philosophical step for some. But in terms of public policy, it represents *only a small step beyond charter schools*, a change in degree rather than kind."[11] In Milwaukee, voucher advocates pushed the legislation through on the promise that it would be limited to low-income students in the public schools. But after seven years, the Milwaukee Parental Choice Program reported only modest numbers of public school families using vouchers. Milwaukee's mayor, John Nordquist, proposed that the income limits (175 percent of official poverty) be lifted to permit all families to receive public funding for their private school bills.

Universal Vouchers and Poor City Children

Without exception, research establishes a high correlation between very low income and low academic achievement. A child whose unmarried mother hasn't finished high school, has little or no work experience, and lives in dependent poverty amid a concentration of neighbors with the same profile is a child doomed to fail society's expectations for literacy and social competency. This underclass has remained reasonably stable for a generation, concentrated in relatively few cities. What has changed is that their neighborhoods are now less crowded as working- and middle-class neighbors flee to safer places with better schools.

The argument for vouchers almost always begins with a recitation of the failure of "government" schools to serve the needs of these poor, overwhelmingly minority students. And, of course, there are plenty of discouraging stories to tell. A typical dirge: "After doing everything educators claim is needed to increase student achievement—reducing class sizes, lowering teacher workloads, hiking teacher pay, and dramatically increasing per-pupil spending—Kansas City has learned the hard way than none of it works."[12] Or consider the words of the Heritage Foundation's journal editor writing about Title I of the Elementary and Secondary Education Act: "This $8 billion annual disaster has spent over $100 billion since its inception in 1965. Its catastrophic result: 57 percent of central-city fourth graders cannot read."[13]

Without the failures of public schools in old cities, voucher advocates have no argument. Suburban parents tend to be reasonably satisfied with the quality of their schools.[14] (In fact, for many suburban families the quality of the local schools is the deciding factor in where to live—ask any suburban realtor.) The proponents of market solutions are relentless, one-sided, and simplistic in their attacks on city schools. Consider the tone of Polly Williams, the heroine of the Right who sponsored the Milwaukee Parental Choice Program in the Wisconsin legislature:

> "The way I saw it," Williams recalls, "the system is preparing our children for slavery. Look at the situation: Drop out by tenth grade, get into the street life—when you should be walking across that stage getting a diploma, you're standing in front of a judge wearing chains."

Parental Choice "is the difference between empowerment and enslavement," Williams told a gathering. . . . "We gotta fight. I'll be the one leading the revolt to destroy the system."[15]

It is ironic that conservative activists have become as interested as they have in the fate of poor, minority children. One is reminded that the very first publicly financed parental choice program was instituted in Virginia with the sole and flamboyant purpose of eviscerating the intent and impact of the *Brown v. Board of Education* decision, and that it was supported by the spiritual and intellectual ancestors of today's voucher proponents.

Large Voucher Programs in Other Fields

What happens when government creates a market by providing money to the very poor—the underclass—and how well are the lofty public goals of those programs served by such expenditures? It is a fair question. Over the last generation, the nation has spent a couple of trillion dollars on various vouchers, many of which have gone to the very poor directly. What can we learn from these substantial and expensive experiences?

The largest voucher program is Medicaid. Administered and cofinanced by the fifty states, Medicaid finances health care for 35 million Americans at an annual (1998) cost of $130 billion. One-third of the money is spent for nursing home patients, about one-fourth for welfare families.

For most of its existence, Medicaid operated as a voucher plan under which welfare recipients selected their own fee-for-service doctor, clinic, or hospital. The health care provider was then reimbursed based on a published payment schedule.

The term *Medicaid mills* has entered the lexicon to describe the fraudulent industry that developed around the new access to taxpayer dollars. Mills are high-volume, paper-shuffling clinics and labs that exploit the good faith of unsophisticated patients to defraud the government of money intended to meet the health needs of the very poor. Health vouchers, which allow poor persons to select their own health care providers, are essential to this theft of public funds.

The mills are not found everywhere. They are concentrated among the poor along with the cash-checking service, the "academy of beauty culture," the credit dentist, the storefront church, the spartan ethnic take-out, and the corner tavern. Their victims are the mothers of the children who are the supposed beneficiaries of school vouchers.

The bipartisan answer to these mills? Narrow the consumer choices offered poor patients by funneling them into a few HMOs. By June 1997, almost half (48 percent) of welfare recipients were in managed care (up from 10 percent in 1991). By establishing a handful of gatekeepers, state governments may reduce the number of vendors to be audited, but there is no evidence yet that constricting the choices of poor persons improves on the production-line character of the health care they receive.

The vouchers that most closely parallel proposals for schools are those that provide funds directly to individuals for postsecondary education via federal grants and loans. The undeniable success of the GI Bill of Rights, Pell grants, and Stafford loans are integral to the arguments of voucher proponents, particularly as a counter to church-state worries. After all, advocates observe, any vet was free to use his GI grant to attend Notre Dame or Virginia, Yeshiva or Boston University. Few argue with the beneficial results of these federal grant and loan programs, which have enabled millions of poor and working-class Americans to obtain a college education as their ticket to middle-class status.

By 1997, the federal government was spending $35 billion in direct assistance to postsecondary students (out of $200 billion in college and university spending). The creation of this very large market led to the systematic theft of public funds on a grand scale. Most of the money was taken by proprietary trade school operators, who once again exploited the putative beneficiaries of elementary and secondary school vouchers—the city poor.

Unscrupulous trade schools invest in wholesale marketing and advertising directed at the least sophisticated consumers, who are promised "free" training leading to "glamorous, high-paying jobs." The shabby downtowns of many cities are landmarked with "cosmetology academies" and "beauticians' institutes." Primary emphasis is placed on advertising, sales (commissioned salespeople were finally outlawed in 1992), and handling the paperwork for federal funds. One school, the American Career Training Corp. in Florida, employed 109 recruiters, 70 financial aid officers, but just 23 instructors.[16] Poor Americans have been falsely and knowingly promised jobs that don't exist and given worthless training at taxpayer expense. For example, even though there are about 1 million unemployed cosmetologists, proprietary trade schools continue to enroll 200,000 or so new students each year—with federal taxpayers standing behind about $725 million in new loans.[17] When the jobs do not materialize, "graduates" are unable to repay their loans and the taxpayers are stuck. At some trade schools, two-thirds of loan recipients have defaulted.

No sector of postsecondary education relies as heavily on federal loans and grants—80 percent of all trade school students received some or all of their tuition from federal taxpayers.[18] The annual taxpayer loss on loan defaults from trade schools runs in the $1.5 to $2.0 billion range. The "loss" from wasted Pell grants is more difficult to estimate, but could easily run $500 million a year. Herein lies a tale pertinent to the push for vouchers: Profits drive markets, even when the demand is created by public funding, and then the profit motive overwhelms the intended public benefits.

The market for postsecondary schools is thinly regulated. Vouchers are paid to anyone who meets the income qualifications and is accepted by an accredited institution. Proprietary trade schools accredit themselves through an association that relies on the dues and fees of those who are already accredited—a blatant conflict of interest. In the process, accreditors shut out potential nonprofit competitors.

One can expect that elementary and secondary school vouchers will draw in the same kind of operators who employ exploitative merchandising of shabby trade schools. For-profit or proprietary elementary and secondary schools have not been operating long enough to reach any definite conclusions (before the early 1990s, the only proprietary schools were limited to preschool and kindergarten and specialized services for handicapped students). In the unregulated marketplace contemplated by voucher advocates, we can expect the "Royal College of Cosmetology" to open a subsidiary, "The Oxbridge Centre of Fyne Schooling."

Efficient and fair markets require that information about products and services be freely available to diligent and rational consumers. Unfortunately, some markets are constructed on precisely opposite assumptions about the capacity and sophistication of the consumer. Voucher proponents ignore the extensive and costly experiences of Medicaid and proprietary trade schools. Instead, they insist that market forces will sort out good schools from bad and that that process requires no oversight from intrusive government regulators.

The Profit Motive and School Improvement

In Milton Friedman's world, entrepreneurs replace educational bureaucrats and there is a new McSchool in every neighborhood. Over time, public schools as we know them would wither away, unable to match their more nimble competitors in quality, innovation, or efficiency. Rose Friedman stated in a 1999 interview: "We would like to see parents being responsible for the education of their children and not the government."[19] Already, with just a few hundred proprietary schools in operation, Milton Friedman concludes that "old methods of teaching are being rapidly replaced by newer methods that are surviving the test of the market." And "costs are going down at the same time that quality is going up."[20]

Friedman's victory declaration is premature and wildly exaggerated. Only about 100,000 children—out of 50 million—attend proprietary elementary and secondary schools (a big plurality in preschool programs). The largest corporate operator of early childhood centers and elementary schools, Nobel Education Dynamics, ignores city neighborhoods altogether. It targets families with two working spouses in middle-income suburbs by providing educationally oriented child care beginning at age two, clustering sufficient early-childhood centers to create the base for elementary schools and, eventually, for middle schools. The emphasis is on convenience (6:30 A.M. to 6:30 P.M.), technology-aided instruction, small class size (17:1 student to teacher ratios), and neighborhood orientation. Savings are generated by clustering, avoiding special needs children, and standardizing facilities, supplies, and curriculum. Nobel's approach may be effective and attractive to customers, but it is hardly a dazzling breakthrough in instruction, quality, or costs.

Moreover, when corporations focus on city schools, Friedman's thesis is badly weakened. Educational Alternatives, Inc., (EAI) was in the business of taking over public schools with the promise that, for much less money, the academic performance of students would improve noticeably and quickly. EAI contracted to run one school in Miami in 1990, twelve schools in Baltimore in 1991, and the entire Hartford school system of 24,000 students in thirty-two schools in 1994. Wall Street responded by driving EAI's stock price up to $48.75 a share in 1993.

By early 1996, EAI had been kicked out of all three cities, and its stock price had plummeted to $4. Dade County did not renew its contract after five years because there was "no significant difference" in student performance in the EAI-managed school when compared to performance in comparable schools elsewhere in the district.[21] Baltimore canceled its contract with EAI in the fourth year of a five-year contract because EAI would not reduce its fees.[22] Hartford officials complained that EAI had failed to produce the promised savings—and therefore canceled the contract after only two years.[23]

In EAI's case, the stock market was an excellent appraiser of how well one private company delivered on its flamboyant promises to "turn around" tough city schools and save the taxpayers money at the same time. In 1997, EAI resurrected itself, changed its name to TesseracT Group, and focused on developing proprietary schools as a part of major housing developments in Arizona. Its losses widened, its senior executives were fired (except for the CEO/chairman), and its stock price hovered in the $2 to $6 range.

EAI's record sends a clear warning that the profit incentive by itself is not enough to solve the educational problems that have bedeviled the nation for decades. Proprietary schools have no special answers when they switch from educating children of the middle and upper-middle classes to educating poor kids in cities.

Is There Room in the Private Schools?

In the rosy scenarios painted by voucher proponents, students from grim, "industrial" public schools transform their lives by transferring to clean, safe, purposeful private schools. With full-scale voucher programs, what kinds of schools would participate and who would benefit? As we learned in Mr. Bolick's opening tale, the prestigious and selective independent schools want no part of vouchers. In the unlikely event that they were amenable, the public would not tolerate taxpayer funds subsidizing tuitions in the $15,000 to $18,000 stratosphere.

This leaves relatively few nonselective independent schools and religious schools to fill the expected demand. Based on the only large-scale surveys of the question, voucher proponents are likely to be disappointed.

A 1993 California referendum called "Parental Choice in Education" proposed that every child in the state receive a $2,600 voucher. Expecting a favorable vote (the referendum was, in fact, defeated), the Southwest Regional Laboratory surveyed all eligible private schools. Nearly a thousand schools replied (37 percent of the statewide universe), reflecting quite closely the composition of all private schools by affiliation, grade levels, enrollment, and location.[24] The survey found that there would be practically no room for voucher students. The only certain beneficiaries would be the parents of children already attending private schools and operators of marginal schools with lots of empty seats. Less than half of respondent schools said that it was "very likely" that they would accept voucher students; a quarter said that it was in fact unlikely. But 40 percent of the "very likely" schools reported that they were already operating at peak capacity (meaning 95 percent or higher). When the capacity of other schools was included, the authors of the survey analysis projected openings for fewer than 39,000 additional nonpublic students statewide.[25] Being extremely optimistic by assuming that 40 percent of the two thousand or so receptive schools would double their capacities within a reasonably short period of time, the authors estimated that 4 percent of the public school enrollment could be accommodated.[26]

At the same time, a second poll—by the Reason Foundation—found that over half of the parents in the Los Angeles city schools would use the proposed voucher. Reason extrapolated that as many as 2.7 million students statewide would seek to enroll in private schools (versus the then-current enrollment of about 500,000).[27] Assuming that Reason overstated the likely response by a factor of three, its survey still portended finding places for 900,000 new students—a far cry from the available seats.

But limited capacity is not the only barrier to universal vouchers. Even among Catholic schools—the most egalitarian of private schools—there were other high barriers to participation. Cost would be a factor only for the poorest families; the proposed $2,600 voucher would cover the tuition at most Catholic elementary schools and would make Catholic secondary schools affordable for most public school families. However, more than 10 percent of public school students are classified as disabled, and Catholic schools typically offer no special education programs. Fewer than 5 percent of Catholic schools offer English instruction, even though California has the largest number of non-English-speaking students in the nation. And finally, 88 percent of Catholic schools require that entering students perform at grade level on standardized entrance examinations.[28]

Based on available space, a universal voucher program in California would have practically no effect on public school enrollments. That is, fewer than 2 percent of public school students could find their way into private schools of any kind if vouchers were approved. The promise, then, is one of frustration for parents who are anxious to see such programs enacted with the hope that their children will benefit.

The U.S. Department of Education conducted a major survey to determine if nonpublic schools would offer their empty places to students from overcrowded public schools. Given its dramatic results, surprisingly little attention has been given this comprehensive study of nonpublic-school capacity.

Twenty-two cities with a self-defined overcrowding problem were surveyed along with most religious and nonsectarian independent schools within commuting distance. The preliminary results showed that, indeed, in some cities, such as Pittsburgh, New Orleans, and Houston (all experiencing enrollment declines or very modest growth), the entire surplus of public school students could be accommodated in private schools.[29] In faster-growing districts such as Dade County and San Diego, private schools would hardly make a difference. (And the total number of places available nationally would barely satisfy New York's growing needs—if they were all in New York!)

What is directly on point for the voucher debate is the sharp falloff in private school participation once certain public objectives are described. If private schools had to accept students by random assignment, the number of definite or probable places would fall from 134,000 to 63,000 (one respondent replied "NOT interested!!" to clarify the position of a group of Christian schools).[30] Only 41,000 places would be available if special needs students were a part of the mix. If public school students transferring in had the right to exempt themselves from religious observances, only 33,000 spots would be offered.[31] In fact, the largest nonpublic-school associations (Roman Catholic, Lutheran, and Christian) were very clear in their rejection of such a request. The Christian Schools International said, "Our schools would not allow the exemption because every class is permeated with a Christian religious viewpoint."[32]

It is not even certain that educational quality would be improved by taking advantage of nonpublic vacancies. One should be alarmed that 53 percent of the available places are offered by private schools that are operating at less than 70 percent capacity.[33]

As in the California survey, the space available in the twenty-two cities surveyed by the U.S. Department of Education—assuming no conditions are imposed—is less than 4 percent of the public school enrollments. And in fast-growing city school systems such as Miami, San Diego, and New York (where many students speak little English and many others have special needs), the few available spaces would do very little good as they would at best skim off the most easily educated of the school population, leaving the rest behind (assuming public schools would allow private schools to select which students could transfer out of crowded schools—a dubious assumption).

The implications of the federal survey for programs such as Florida's Opportunity Scholarship program, passed with great fanfare in 1999, are overwhelmingly negative. Governor Jeb Bush's legislation is conditioned on random assignment of students seeking to leave those public schools classified by the state as failing.[34] The Florida law does not allow students to exempt themselves from religious instruction.

Excluding Poor Kids Is Un-American

We end where we began, with attention focused on the needs and rights of poor children attending dysfunctional public schools. After reviewing all the reasons for doubt—and there are many—we come back to what is not only a policy or theoretical or political question, but one of morality and fairness. Should any parents be made to accept an unequal, low-quality education for their child on the basis that the child's removal from a public school classroom will possibly reduce the performance of the children of uninterested parents who will be left behind? We can't be certain of the effects of so-called strivers exiting public schools. We can't be certain that large numbers of them can even be accommodated by decent private schools. If they get there, we can't be certain that they'll do any better academically than they might have at their old school.

So what? Before accepting a radical policy that—by definition—undercuts the civic values served by public schools, should we not have some greater assurance on these issues than has been mustered to date? In fact, as we have shown, most of the evidence increases one's level of doubt about the voucher proposition rather than satisfying it.

At some point public authority must respond to low-income parents who want the same thing for their children that all the voucher opponents and advocates want for theirs. On an individual basis, how can one deny parents the right to pursue every alternative for their child? The public schools must deliver on their responsibilities—and not at some distant point in the future—or parents should be given the means of escape. Public charter schools are established to operate (and usually do) as open-enrollment schools offering variety, focus, and a freedom from regulation not found in public district schools. Charter schools address both the issues of failed district schools and parental choice without obliterating the civic virtue of the common school.

Voucher proponents must account for their persistence in the face of overwhelming evidence that the capacity of good nonpublic schools to absorb dissatisfied students from public schools is extremely modest. They should respond to the growing evidence that the overwhelming majority of nonpublic schools do not want to accept the poorest students, the ones whose English is halting, or those with disabilities. And the 85 percent of nonpublic schools that are religious will not and should not deny their religious purposes simply to receive tax funds. The crusade to subsidize religious instruction in the guise of helping a few poor students in failed public schools is, in the end, cynical.

To be acceptable to the American public, any voucher program should impose one requirement, a requirement that most private schools and voucher proponents currently ignore: Voucher schools must accept students randomly, even if such acceptance means that their (religious) vision of themselves is qualified and diluted. Otherwise, tax dollars will be used to create intentionally exclusionary systems of schooling that are—what else?—un-American.

THE PROBLEM WITH PRIVATE SCHOOL TAX EXEMPTIONS

RICHARD C. LEONE

In October 1997, the House of Representatives took time out from beating up the Internal Revenue Service to approve a fresh tax loophole. The proposal would authorize households to use up to $2,500 of after-tax money to establish "school" accounts, whose earnings would be tax free if used for certain education-related purposes.

Lots of silly numbers were thrown around during the debate, but common sense tells us that the measure's promise for most taxpayers isn't just hollow, it's trivial. For the 80 percent of families with incomes of less than $50,000 a year, the payoff in tax savings would probably be a princely $15 a year or less—not much of a down payment on the private school tuition, home computers, and such that would be among the permitted uses for the money. Indeed, $15 won't even buy a school uniform. Realistically, the full tax benefit of the school account could be captured only by someone whose income was close to the bill's highest allowable level, $95,000, and who was a consistently lucky investor. Such people, of course, are the ones whose children are most likely to attend private schools; the 90 percent of American children who go to public schools would not be helped significantly.

These arguments, however, are seldom persuasive in Washington because they ignore the underlying explanation for the complexity of the tax code: most tax benefits reward those who vote regularly and, even more important, contribute to campaigns. Tax breaks are always

Originally published as "A Not-So-Innocent Tax Exemption" in the *New York Times*, October 28,1997. Reprinted by permission.

worth more the higher your tax bracket. With a rate of 15 percent, a $1,000 tax deduction is worth $150; for those in the 40 percent bracket, it's worth $400.

Of course, we expect the rich to reap rewards for their political largess. But this innocent-sounding little exemption would become a real danger if it were made bigger. And it is just one piece of the agenda of privatization now being pushed by the right—an agenda that offers false choices and seeks to shrink the public and community sphere, further dividing the haves and the have-nots.

The school accounts now being proposed are cousins of individual health accounts that will compete with Medicare, proposals to create private accounts to replace all or part of Social Security, and other every-man-for-himself ideas so popular on the right. In each case, those with the largest incomes, the best health, or the most wealth can opt out of the national mechanism for sharing risk and responsibility.

Supporters of the school-accounts idea insist that it would provide new choices for average families. Nonsense. How could the tiny tax savings for most families provide the crucial margin in decisions about private versus public schools? All that this new loophole would do is help those whose children already attend private school to stay there.

More generally, it would reinforce the notion that education is something to be bought, to be bid on. This is its most damaging feature, for when each of us buys our own education, will all of us get enough?

We all have a stake in an educated citizenry, even if we don't have children in school. Public schools, after all, are not some radical new idea. Nor is the notion of a national insurance program for the elderly. They are the glue that makes us one people. They, like fair taxes, reflect our shared interest in community and one another.

Those in the monied class already are insulated from the rest of America. That's their choice; that's capitalism. But let's at least try to keep them involved in the most basic of civic enterprises, public education.

3.

Myth #1: Vouchers Raise Student Achievement

The Early Research on School Vouchers

Gordon MacInnes

Achievement: Will Private Schools Do a Better Job?

Voucher advocates assume that private schools are almost always superior to public schools. They are, after all, free of the suffocating bureaucracy that crushes creativity and imposes thoughtless demands on principals and teachers. They are smaller than public schools. They are usually organized for a specific purpose, most frequently to inculcate the religious doctrines of a particular denomination or sect. They benefit from what researchers call "selection bias"—the fact that they accept only the children of parents who care enough about education to, at a minimum, pay a private school tuition. Test results inevitably show that students in private schools outperform students in public schools. That is, on average, most of the time, for most students.

Here, however, we care about what happens to poor city kids, not to their affluent suburban counterparts. When differences in student

---

Excerpts from Gordon MacInnes, "Kids Who Pick the Wrong Parents and Other Victims of Voucher Schemes," The Century Foundation, New York, 1999.

background are considered, most research shows that the private school advantage is wiped out.

The pathbreaking research that deals with the largest number of students from both sectors over the longest period of time, connecting individual students to specific classroom teachers, was conducted by Dan Goldhaber. Using data from the National Educational Longitudinal Study of 1988, Goldhaber had social and economic information not only on individual students, their families, and classmates (as opposed to "blind" aggregates), but also on their teachers. In addition, he had the advantage of tests offered in four subject areas in both the eighth and tenth grades. His analysis of the math and reading test results leads to this conclusion: "*In no case is there a positive statistically significant sectoral effect favoring private schools*. Hence the argument that the private sector outperforms the public appears weak."[1] Goldhaber asserts that he has corrected for selection bias by using achievement models that use the tenth-grade results as a function of eighth-grade achievement, the student–family profile, and school differences (for example, class size), as well as a factor for parent choice.[2]

Although he acknowledges that in the real world *ceteris paribus* is rarely achieved, Goldhaber concludes that "*with a given set of schooling resources, there is no reason to believe that an average private school would do a better job of educating a group of students than an average public school educating that same group of students*."[3] Of course, an on-the-ground test of Goldhaber's proposition cannot be arranged, and parents will be given choices where the school resources will not be equal. (For affluent parents the resources will almost always be superior at the private school; this is not always the case for lower-income parents.)

The belief that nonpublic schools are better for poor kids was strengthened by the conclusions published in a highly visible work by the author of the *Coleman Report*, James S. Coleman, and two others, in which private high schools, particularly Catholic schools, were presented as being highly effective compared to public schools.[4] Subsequent analysis, which controlled for "selection bias" and corrected problems in statistical design, greatly reduced or eliminated the private school advantage. Henry Levin found in a 1987 study that, in fact, almost half of "public school students have *higher* achievement than the average private school student who is statistically similar."[5]

There is one area where Catholic high schools appear to enjoy an advantage over public high schools: graduation and college attendance rates for disadvantaged Latinos and blacks. Derek Neal concludes that the fact that Latino and black graduation rates from Catholic city high schools is 13 percent to 26 percent higher than from public schools is best explained by the very low rates found in public high schools.[6]

What explains these putative advantages? In a 1993 follow-on to the work of Coleman and his colleagues, Anthony Bryk and two others argued that Catholic high schools (their study excluded elementary schools) are able to do better for three basic reasons. First, Catholic schools focus on academics, and all students are expected to take a solid schedule of relatively challenging academic courses to the exclusion of many of the "soft" course-offerings found in the general track in public high schools. Second, discipline is much better, made easier by the fact that troublesome students can be (and are) expelled. Third, Catholic schools benefit from a sense of community they create among clergy, parents, and students. The religious and academic missions breed a shared sense of purpose and cohesion not found in large, "shopping mall" high schools.[7]

The private-versus-public debate most recently has centered on conflicting claims from the Milwaukee voucher program, to which we now turn.

Learning from Milwaukee

The nation's first, broadest, and largest voucher experiment is taking place in Milwaukee. As such, it deserves the scrutiny of anyone interested in vouchers. The program is highly controversial for predictable reasons—it threatens the idea of the "common school," it leaves the students with the toughest social and educational problems to the public schools, it takes badly needed funds from public school programs that work, and it uses tax funds for religious indoctrination. To intensify feelings, the debate has been marked by bitter personal exchanges between the two scholars most prominent in efforts to assess its educational effectiveness.

The Milwaukee Parental Choice Program (MPCP) was started in 1990 and was restricted to nonsectarian private schools. Only students from families with incomes below 175 percent of the official poverty rate ($28,788 for a family of four) are eligible.

MPCP grew slowly in its first seven years, starting with 337 choice students in September 1990 and climbing to 1,501 in 1997—always well short of the statutory ceiling, which rose from 1 percent of enrollment of the Milwaukee public schools in 1990 (or 931 students) to 7 percent (about 6,500) in 1995.[8] Attrition rates were high, averaging about 30 percent each year.

The number of participating independent schools grew from seven in 1990 to twenty-three in 1997 (but never included the Sidwell-like preparatory schools). Along the way, seven schools either closed or dropped out of the program.

In 1995, MPCP was amended at Governor Tommy Thompson's urging to permit students to select religious schools and to increase the ceiling on choice enrollments from 7 to 15 percent of Milwaukee's public school "membership." The paperwork required of participating schools and the oversight by the state department of education were streamlined, so that the statute could avoid being overturned under the "entanglement" test imposed by the U.S. Supreme Court in *Lemon v. Krutzman* (1971). The inclusion of religious schools was challenged unsuccessfully in the Wisconsin Supreme Court by the American Civil Liberties Union, People for the American Way, and the National Education Association. In October 1998, the U.S. Supreme Court refused to hear their appeal.

In September 1998, the number of participating schools jumped from twenty-three to eighty-seven, including seven additional nonsectarian schools and fifty-seven religious schools (forty of forty-five Catholic schools joined).

Whereas a maximum of about 15,000 of Milwaukee's 104,000 students could opt for nonpublic schools (70,000 are estimated to qualify by income), the September 1998 enrollment was 5,825 (on a full-time equivalent basis), of whom 791 (13.6 percent) were four- and five-year-old kindergartners; 2,328 (40 percent) *had already been attending the newly eligible religious schools* in 1997–98; 1,327 (22.8 percent) had continued from the 1997–98 Choice program; and 1,379 (23.6 percent) had transferred from Milwaukee public schools. Preliminary figures for 1999 show that an additional 1,900 students have switched to nonpublic schools through the program, meaning that about 4,600 students have left Milwaukee public schools after eight years.

Given the bullish predictions by voucher proponents that low-income parents would jump at the chance to leave public schools, the most striking statistic is that less than 5 percent of eligible parents took advantage of the new opportunities to take their children out of public schools at no cost.

This result clashes sharply with the experience reported by the Children's Scholarship Fund (CSF), which claimed that the low-income parents of 1.2 million students applied for just 40,000 privately financed scholarships. CSF's cofounder Ted Forstmann declared the debate over in a "thunderous demonstration of dissatisfaction with the present system."[9] There is a huge difference, of course. First, some large number of applicants and recipients for CSF grants were already in nonpublic schools (30 percent in Philadelphia, for example).[10] Moreover, there was unchecked encouragement for applications (which came from all fifty states and 21,960 ineligible municipalities) with no screening for income. CSF was more in the nature of a sweepstakes contest or lottery with no consequences for entering; by contrast, the Milwaukee program requires parents to identify a specific school and proceed through a rigorous application process.

Are Poor Kids Better Educated in Milwaukee's Private Schools?

The search for an answer to this question has set off an ideological and highly personal battle between two seasoned scholars and their respective camps.

John Witte, a University of Wisconsin-Madison political scientist, was selected by the state superintendent of education to conduct the evaluation of the MPCP. Through the first five years of the program, he issued annual assessments with recommendations (at which point, the Wisconsin legislature terminated the evaluation). In general, he found that MPCP was meeting many of its statutory objectives, but that it was not clear that choice students were benefiting educationally over their peers who stayed behind in the Milwaukee Public Schools (MPS). He summarized his findings this way:

> The Milwaukee choice program is clearly successful in providing some families with an opportunity to attend alternative schools that they would be hard pressed to afford otherwise. The students come from poor and working-class families, and they have not done well in their prior public schools. To the extent that the purpose of the program is to create these opportunities, the program is succeeding.[11]

Witte found that choice parents were slightly poorer than a control panel of low-income parents with children in the Milwaukee Public Schools, more dissatisfied with those schools, and more active on behalf of their children. They also were better educated (53 percent reporting "some college") than MPS parents of low income (30 percent of whom reported "some college"), and headed significantly smaller families (2.63 children in choice families versus 3.24 in the MPS control group).[12]

Witte also found that choice parents were much more active in the voucher schools than they had been in the MPS and more active than their demographic peers who stayed behind. Choice parents were also very satisfied with MPCP.[13]

The performance on standardized tests by choice students once in their nonpublic schools defies easy generalization. Witte summarized his findings in these terms:

> Choice students' reading scores increased the first year, fell substantially in the second year, and have remained approximately the same in the next three years. Because the sample size was very small in the first year, the gain . . . was not statistically significant, but the decline in the second year was. In math, choice students were essentially the same in the first two years, recorded a significant increase in the third year, and then significantly declined.[14]

In short, *choice students did not perform appreciably better or worse than students of low income who stayed in the* MPS. When controlled for the education level of the mother, reading scores for choice students were *negative* contrasted with their MPS peers. As to tentatively higher math scores, Witte cites high attrition rates (averaging over 30 percent in each of the first five years), leaving the choice schools with a residue of particularly well-motivated students as marginal performers returned to public schools.[15]

Paul Peterson of Harvard disagreed early, often, vociferously, and strongly with Witte's evaluation. He challenged Witte's appointment by the antivoucher state superintendent, Herbert Grover, whose "eagerness to move quickly [with the appointment] jeopardized his ability to obtain a high-quality evaluation."[16] He challenged Witte's objectivity: "Witte was hardly disinterested. . . . He had written a paper, *well received in teacher-union circles*, which criticized studies finding private schools outperforming public schools."[17] He characterized Witte's evaluation as "immediate, if inept."[18] And he attacked Witte's scholarly competence: "Witte's criticism [of Peterson] reveals a lack of knowledge about the way in which one appropriately analyzes data from a randomized experiment."[19]

Even when Witte is citing evidence as straightforward as attrition rates, Peterson criticizes him as "wrong" for saying that annual rates of 46 percent, 35 percent, 31 percent, 27 percent, and 28 percent were "high." Why? Because compared to mobility rates at Milwaukee's low-income public schools, the rates represent an improvement.[20]

Peterson and his colleagues find that Milwaukee choice students "made substantial gains." In math tests, "choice students scored, on average, 5 percentile points higher than nonselected students in year three and over 11 points higher in year four." (Nonselected students in Peterson's study were those who applied to the three most popular schools—one Latino, two black—but were not accepted in the random lottery.) In reading, "choice students scored, on average, 3 percentile points higher after three years than those not selected."[21] Peterson estimates that if similar gains could be made nationwide, the gap between minority and white test scores would close by "one-third to one-half."[22]

Our purpose (or competence) is not to resolve the methodological or personal disputes between Witte and Peterson, but to approximate the truth on the question of educational results. Cecilia Rouse of Princeton, who evaluated the evaluations, agrees with Witte that there is no significant difference in reading rates, and with Peterson that choice students made gains in math while their public school peers declined (the relative differential in math scores is mostly explained by MPS declines).[23] In addition to this comparison of choice student scores with those of all MPS students, Rouse also compared choice student scores with those of students attending citywide magnet schools and with the 25 percent of MPS elementary students who attend so-called P–5 schools—a state-mandated and financed program that involves frequent testing, smaller class sizes, and teacher training and evaluations. Rouse concludes that P–5 students do as well as choice students in math and noticeably better in reading.[24]

One of the strongest and most frequent arguments advanced by voucher advocates maintains that the mere threat of taxpayer subsidies for private and religious schools will force public schools to compete and to improve to meet the potential loss of students and, not incidentally, state aid. Nothing else will work, they suggest, short of an end to the public school monopoly. The MPS have taken notice, at least in a cosmetic way. MPS's new strategic plan sets as its first objective maintaining student achievement against high standards and, as its second, making Milwaukee's public schools the first choice of steadily growing numbers of parents. MPS is expanding the P–5 program and now guarantees that parents signing a contract will see their second grader read on grade level. There is no way to tell if these laudable objectives are suffusing the activities of individual schools and classrooms. Until there is controlled research that contrasts educational achievement by Milwaukee's "stay-behinds" after vouchers were initiated with comparable students in non-voucher cities, the competing claims cannot be sorted out.

Recent Evidence on the Effectiveness of School Voucher Programs

Bernard Wasow

As we struggle to improve our education system, we must move with care. An educational experiment puts in play not only current participants and their communities but future generations, whose teachers are today's students. We must review a variety of options and learn as much as we can about the likely costs and benefits. In spite of these obvious caveats, the effort to promote school vouchers has been buttressed with relatively little evidence regarding the results of the voucher programs that have been undertaken so far. Further study is hampered, too, by the fact that public schools are required to provide test results to demonstrate students' progress but private schools generally are not. What evidence we have is not encouraging to those who see in vouchers a magic bullet. At best, participation in voucher programs has raised test scores a small amount, and even this may well be attributable simply to the effects of class size.

Why Effects Are Hard to Measure

Results of voucher programs are hard to measure for two main reasons:

1. How should success be defined?

The author would like to thank Caroline Hoxby, Cecilia Rouse, Julie Cullen, Martin Carnoy, and Alan Krueger for their cooperation and help. All opinions in this essay are the author's alone, not those of the people who aided him nor of The Century Foundation.

2. How can the effect of vouchers be disentangled from other causes of success, such as the student's social circumstances or differences between the motivation of those who seek vouchers and those who do not?

The success of our education system can only be gauged if we are clear about what it is supposed to deliver. We certainly want graduates who have mastered skills. But it also is obvious that we want more from our graduates than literacy, numeracy, and job skills. Why else would we build a curriculum that includes history, civics, literature, and gym? We want our schools to produce cooperative citizens who contribute to the ongoing American effort to build one nation out of diverse components. And our success at this is hard to measure through testing, as socialization plays out over a lifetime. Civic engagement, participation in community activities, and responsible parenthood all can be influenced by experiences in school. If our schools produced graduates who read well but only read the holy books of their own religion, the social cohesion of America might be jeopardized even as reading test scores rose.

What about parental satisfaction as an indicator of success? Results of voucher experiments in the United States show that the majority of voucher recipients who are allowed to do so attend religious schools.[1] In New Zealand, the introduction of vouchers led to an increase in segregation by race and class. In Chile, where vouchers have been widely used for twenty years, there has been similar sorting of students among schools by social class.[2] Parents' decision to use vouchers in this way shows that this is what they want. But surely society needs more out of publicly funded education than satisfied parents, particularly if the reason for parental satisfaction is that their children now can use tax dollars to attend school with children only of their own religion, race, or class.

Some proponents of vouchers argue for their desirability simply by comparing the results of public versus private school education. School vouchers may be a new idea, but private schooling surely is not, and if private school graduates do better in life than public school graduates, some take this as a prima facie case for the superiority of private education. The problem with such comparisons is that public and private schools are fundamentally distinct: private schools serve populations with different socioeconomic characteristics from public schools; they serve motivated parents who seek them out; and, probably most important, they determine whom they will admit and retain. To state the last point another way, public schools must teach those who are rejected or expelled by private schools.

Other studies look at the performance of voucher recipients compared to public school students who are otherwise similar. The problem with such studies is that the recipients of vouchers and the "control group" can only be matched according to what can be observed. What is more, the control group is surely different from the voucher group in one very important way: most of the control group did not show interest in the voucher program. One can only guess at the consequences of having parents who sought out a voucher program.

Good evidence on the success of voucher programs, as opposed to the casual or flawed empiricism of comparing public and private schools or their students, could come from an experiment in which a randomly selected part of a homogeneous population received vouchers and the remainder did not. The differences in outcomes for the two groups should then be tracked over time. Several studies have come close to this ideal. Because voucher programs often are oversubscribed, vouchers are offered to applicants through a lottery. Everyone in the lottery meets the income and other selection criteria, and every family seeks vouchers. Lottery winners are selected from this population by blind luck. So the losers become the control group.

In spite of these sound methodological plans, however, the actual studies that use such an approach still face a problem. Not all of those who are offered a voucher choose to use it; some go to public school anyway. Among lottery losers, some nevertheless go to a private school, which may not be part of the study. And, over time, there is tremendous turnover as students change schools, move away, or simply fail to continue providing information. While the difference between winners and losers in a lottery for a limited number of vouchers is random, the difference between those who remain in the study and those who do not almost certainly is not random. Since the populations are now different, it cannot be known how much of any variation in educational success owes to schooling and how much to unobservables (such as motivation of the family or unreported resources—such as aid from grandparents—that help pay for private schooling). This problem of "self-selection" becomes greater and greater over time, and it is precisely the long-run effects of vouchers that are of most interest. In fact, according to the U.S. General Accounting Office, private voucher programs (most of which only cover part of the expenses of attending a private school) often have attrition rates of 20 percent per year.[3]

Research Results

There is no voucher plan that fulfills all the requirements for a sound experiment. For one thing, few voucher programs have been tried, and all of these have begun relatively recently. So if one wanted to ask, for example, about the employment, criminal justice, or family formation experiences of those who received vouchers in their youth, there would be no data to draw on.

The best data available on a publicly funded program are from Milwaukee, which has provided vouchers to some disadvantaged students since 1990, initially to attend nonsectarian private schools. Seven private schools participated in the first year, rising to twenty in 1996 and to nearly ninety in 1998, when religious schools were added. If a school had too many voucher applicants (the maximum allowed under the program was 49 percent of enrollment), a lottery was used to choose who would be admitted. Cecilia Rouse of Princeton University has compared the results on standardized tests of the students admitted through such lotteries and those who were not selected from the same lottery pool.[4] Earlier research on the Milwaukee experiment was inconsistent and contentious. In using the losers from the lottery as the control population while also correcting for deviations from randomness in the lottery process, Rouse avoided the issue of comparability that bedeviled earlier studies. She concluded that those selected by private school lotteries gained 1–1.5 percentage points per year on their mathematics test scores but performed the same as the control group on reading tests.

Rouse undertook a follow-up study in which she compared Milwaukee's voucher programs not only to ordinary public schools but also to magnet schools and schools participating in a program for particularly low-performing public schools (P–5 schools).[5] That study suggested that magnet schools performed like ordinary public schools (for the population of voucher seekers) but that P–5 schools performed like voucher schools in generating slight improvements in mathematics test scores while better than voucher schools in generating small increases in reading scores as well. Rouse notes that the relatively good results in the P–5 schools, which received extra funding in return for meeting certain norms for staffing, may be the result of small class size. Other experiments have demonstrated that African American students in smaller classes have slightly better test scores than their peers in larger classes.[6] She conjectures that the advantages of voucher schools, too, may lie in nothing more complicated than smaller classes.

The GAO has surveyed research on results of privately funded voucher experiments.[7] While there are many such experiments currently under way, most are small and lack information good enough to use in an evaluation. Even the research cited in the GAO study—of voucher schemes in New York, Dayton, and Washington, D.C.—is bedeviled by data problems. None of those programs was in existence more than three years when studied, none had more than 1,500 voucher recipients, and all suffered high rates of attrition and inconsistency in test taking. The results, too, hardly invite confidence:[8]

- In New York, African American voucher users (44 percent of the total) performed better on reading tests during all three years of the study and better on math tests two out of three years. Hispanic voucher users (47 percent of the total) performed no differently from the control group. When all groups are pooled, the New York voucher scheme showed no difference in student performance from the control group.

- In Dayton no statistically significant differences in test scores were evident in the two years of data available.

- In Washington, where African Americans constituted 95 percent of voucher recipients, there was no consistent improvement in the test scores of voucher users.

Recently, Alan Krueger has looked more closely at the results for New York, the only ones that show some significant effect of vouchers on test scores, and has called them into question.[9] Krueger reports that when he uses all observations in statistically correct specifications—including observations excluded by William Howell and Paul Peterson because they lacked a baseline test score—the estimated impact of vouchers on African American scores diminishes greatly. Similarly, when he experiments with the definition of race and ethnicity, Krueger finds that results are not robust.[10] It seems that the benefits of vouchers vary inversely with the rigor of the statistical analysis, although some small effects remain for children of non-Hispanic black mothers.

"External" Effects of School Choice

Both proponents and opponents of school vouchers point to effects a system of vouchers might have on students who do not use them at all. Many advocates for school choice—of which voucher programs are one variant—believe that competition for students will force poorly performing schools to do better or face crisis, as families "vote with their feet" to seek education elsewhere. Thus, vouchers could improve the education of not only those who use them but those who are outside the voucher program because the entire school system is forced to meet the challenge of competition. On the other side of the discussion, some opponents of vouchers worry that voucher programs will skim the best and most motivated students off the top of the public school system, leaving behind a peer group of inferior students, reducing the value of education for them all.

Either or both of these conjectures might prove empirically valid (for different programs or different groups), but neither is a hypothesis exclusively about vouchers. Both positive and negative "external" effects are the result of school choice, which could be effected through any of numerous systems in which schools compete for students. School choice could take place entirely within the public school system or outside it; it could involve the school in the selection of whom to admit, or it could use a lottery to determine who attends an oversubscribed school; it could involve all students or a small number. It is possible that each of these variations on school choice would produce different outcomes for students who fail to exercise the options available and remain in their neighborhood schools. In spite of the research results that will be considered below, this is a set of issues that has just begun to be probed.

Evidence on External Effects

So far, the methods employed to evaluate external effects of school choice are fairly rough-and-ready. Most studies measure success by test scores; they measure school choice fairly crudely as well; and most fail to control for variables besides school choice that might affect results. Caroline Hoxby of Harvard University has produced perhaps the most interesting work. Her empirical tests use several approaches.[11] Hoxby first compared school productivity (average percentile ranking on standardized tests per dollar spent) in metropolitan areas differentiated by the degree of school choice within the public schools. Hoxby defines choice as the likelihood that two students within the metropolitan area live in different school districts. Implicitly, she assumes that all choice takes the form of residential sorting; choice does not involve selection among schools within a district. Hoxby reports that metropolitan areas with relatively many school districts produce slightly higher test scores from slightly lower per-student expenditures. In this work, she controls statistically for various socioeconomic differences among metropolitan areas.

Other research on public school choice within metropolitan areas ironically uses an almost contradictory methodology to Hoxby's. Julie Cullen, Brian Jacob, and Steven Levitt of the universities of Michigan and Chicago look at school choice within Chicago.[12] The large number of magnet schools and special career academies for high school students in Chicago are available to them precisely because Chicago is one large school district, in which "parents have an enormous degree of flexibility in choosing which of the more than 60 Chicago Public School high schools their child will attend." In Hoxby's work, a single school district defines *minimum* school choice; in the study by Cullen, Jacob, and Levitt, a single district is the precondition for "an enormous degree of flexibility." The latter also is framed to test the hypothesis that school choice negatively affects the students left behind when others choose to attend special schools. It does not test Hoxby's "rising tide" hypothesis (that competition from special schools increases productivity in neighborhood schools). In spite of these differences, Cullen and her colleagues, like Hoxby, deduce that school choice has no detrimental effects on students who do not participate. Rather, they conclude that the career academies improve the results of students who choose to attend them, while the magnet schools' higher test scores probably simply reflect the unobservable qualities of students who choose to attend them.[13]

Hoxby also looked at the effect of competition with private schools on public school performance. The methodology in this exercise is very similar to her work on public school choice. Her results suggest that public school students in metropolitan areas with more private schools have slightly higher test scores. She does not report results in which her measures of public school choice and private school choice are investigated simultaneously.[14]

Hoxby's most recent set of empirical tests looks at the effect of newly introduced competition on school productivity in three settings: vouchers in Milwaukee and charter schools in Arizona and Michigan. In these tests, she looks at the growth of school productivity before and after the launch of competition. Since these school choice programs all were introduced over time, Hoxby had to define when effective competition began in each case: she posited that Milwaukee vouchers became a competitive threat to public schools in 1998 and that charter schools did so whenever their enrollment passed 6 percent of the school-age population. In Milwaukee, Hoxby found that test scores improved most after 1998 in public schools with the most students eligible for vouchers. In Arizona and Michigan, test scores in public schools grew faster after charter schools passed the stated threshold of challenge. In these statistical tests, Hoxby did not control for other changes in the school system (for example, the introduction of P–5 schools in Milwaukee) because she saw such innovations as responses to the threat of competition.

> When we ask what these schools did to improve between 1998 and 2001, we get a variety of answers (principals being given more control/discretion, bad teachers being "counseled out" because the Milwaukee Public Schools negotiated for this in the contract, special programs, class size). When we look at the *timing* of the changes, there is no doubt that they coincided with the timing of pressure placed on the schools by vouchers. The period when they stood to lose their students (and revenue and jobs) was the period when they suddenly started to improve, after decades of poor and declining performance. When and if public schools react well to vouchers, they *will* do something to improve, so there will always be some program or programs that they can point to. That does not mean that the program would have been implemented or implemented successfully in the absence of vouchers.[15]

Hoxby's hypothesis—that school reform is endogenous and that the introduction of school choice is the only exogenous variable that matters—is plausible, but it has not been adequately tested. In the case of P–5 schools, for example, the hypothesis would have to deal with the fact that the P–5 program was started more than a decade before vouchers were introduced.[16]

CONCLUSION

Some proponents of school vouchers act as if vouchers were a sword to cut the Gordian knot of inferior education for poor children. It is important to recognize that the empirical benefits claimed in the few reviews of the effects of school vouchers that track students over a number of years are at best a few percentage points' improvement on standardized national tests. Even allowing for positive external effects of vouchers (through competitive pressure on ordinary public schools), one might be talking about raising average test scores from the thirtieth to the thirty-fifth or fortieth percentile over a number of years. That is indeed an accomplishment but hardly a breakthrough.

To capture such potential benefits, advocates of privatization are willing to risk substituting for the public education system a private sector that might provide schools similar to the (lower-priced segment of) private schools we have today, or they might offer something quite different. We might get innovative, energetic new educational leaders. Or we might get a rash of hucksters, hustlers, and bigots attracted by the smell of public funds. In all likelihood, we will get both, in an unpredictable mix.

We certainly also would get greater diversity among schools. Disputes that now are aired in debates over public school curriculum—creationism versus science, for example—are likely to become private matters, as parents choose which approach their children will learn. For opponents of vouchers, the prospect of taxpayer support of schools that teach ideas that most scientists regard as nonsense, curricula that promote intolerant religious views, or ethnic chauvinism is frightening; for many, such social and educational side effects of privatization represent a potential cost, not a benefit, of vouchers.

There is little evidence that today's population of private schools can substantially improve the education of students whom the public schools seem to be failing. Apart from parental satisfaction—a questionable criterion, particularly when it involves sectarian education—only slight benefits from vouchers have been demonstrated. What is more, the strongest claims for widespread benefits, claims that require further verification, come through the competitive pressures that school choice places on a system.

These benefits of competition, if future studies confirm that they are real, do not require us to risk the costs that vouchers would impose. We can introduce greater variety in curriculum, along with the inherent incentives of competitive prodding—"shape up or lose your students"—through public school choice. The variety will be less than would be offered in a privatized system (unless regulation of all participating private schools were almost impossibly tight), but public school choice offers the benefits of competition at low risk. The evidence on school voucher programs does not justify abandoning the existing public school system and giving up our faith in the potential of public schools to stir the melting pot. This review of the research to date suggests that many advocates of vouchers have greatly exaggerated the likely benefits, which anyway could be achieved through school choice within the public school system.

The Problem of Taking Private School Voucher Programs to Scale

Richard D. Kahlenberg

The U.S. Supreme Court's decision to permit public funding of vouchers to private religious schools is likely to energize proponents to vastly increase both the number and size of voucher programs. But, ironically, expansion may finally bring to light a central flaw of voucher programs: their ostensible pilot-level successes cannot be replicated when taken to scale. Even if it is true, as voucher proponents claim, that small voucher programs for low-income children increase the achievement of African American students, the best evidence suggests that if those programs were expanded to include much larger numbers of low-income students, the benefits would quickly fade away.

Traditionally, the voucher argument has been fought out on familiar lines. Advocates say it is unfair to trap kids in bad schools; that it is educationally sound to provide more options to children because one size of schooling doesn't fit all students; and that the pressure of competition will improve all schools. Opponents note that under voucher programs, the final "choice" is often given to schools, not to parents; that private schools, accustomed to being independent, are unlikely to comply with public regulation; and that private schools that segment the market on lines of race, religion and ethnic differences will undermine the important role of public schools in promoting democracy, social cohesion, and American citizenship.

But the new court decision in *Zelman v. Simmons-Harris* is likely to raise a fresh set of difficulties for private school voucher advocates: the

---

Originally published as Richard D. Kahlenberg, "The Problem of Taking Private School Voucher Programs to Scale: The Next Issue in the Voucher Wars," Issue Brief, The Century Foundation, New York, 2002.

problem of taking small successes to scale. Some studies have found that private school voucher programs can cut the achievement gap between African American children and whites by nearly one-half after three years, leading proponents like Harvard's Paul Peterson to ask, "Can nine more years or private school education eliminate that test score gap?"[1] But as with many programs that appear to have success on a small-scale level, the evidence suggests that voucher gains are very unlikely to be replicated once programs are expanded to reach large numbers of students. By contrast, this issue brief will argue, public school choice programs, which affect a much larger number of students in the United States than do vouchers (5.8 million vs. 60,000—see Figure 3.1), offer the chance to promote achievement on a grand scale.

FIGURE 3.1 STUDENT PARTICIPATION IN VARIOUS SCHOOL CHOICE PROGRAMS

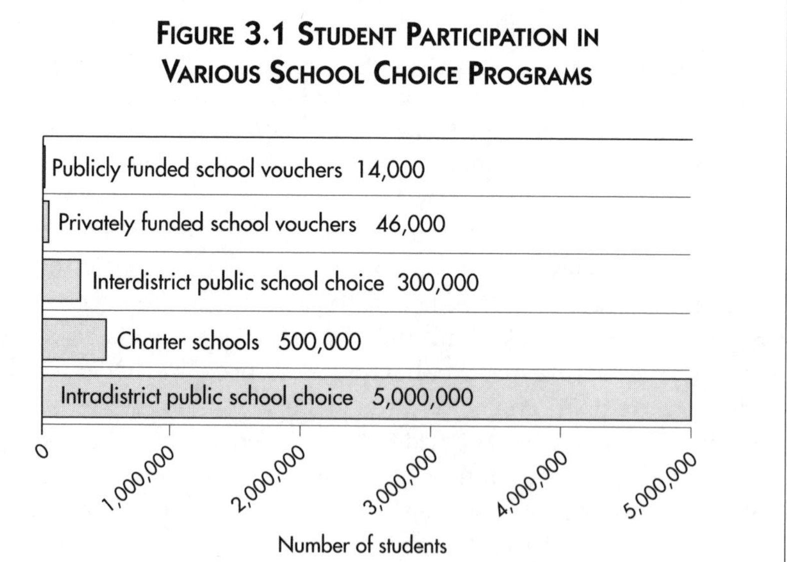

Sources: Jeffrey Henig and Stephen Sugarman, "The Nature and Extent of School Choice," in Stephen Sugarman and Frank Kemerer (Eds), *School Choice and Social Controversy* (Brookings Institution Press, 1999), Table 1-1; William G. Howell and Paul E. Peterson, *The Education Gap: Vouchers and Urban Schools* (Brookings Institution Press, 2002), Table 2-1; Brian P. Gill, P. Michael Timpane, Karen E. Ross, and Dominic J. Brewer, *Rhetoric Versus Reality: What We Know and What We Need to Know about Vouchers and Charter Schools* (Rand, 2001), p. 8.

Recent Voucher Research

The research on vouchers is summarized in two new books, *Rhetoric Versus Reality*, compiled by four Rand researchers, and *The Education Gap*, by the University of Wisconsin's William G. Howell and Paul Peterson.[2] The best studies, both sets of authors agree, involve "randomized field trials." In cities where philanthropists have established privately funded school voucher programs for low-income students—including New York, Washington, and Dayton—many more applications were received than could be accommodated, so lotteries were held to determine which students would receive vouchers. The "treatment group" (those receiving vouchers) is thought to be comparable to the "control group" (those who applied for vouchers but were turned down and remained in public school) because the winners and losers in the lottery are believed to be equally motivated.[3]

Howell and Peterson found that the cumulative average test score change after three years in New York, Washington, and Dayton was a modest 0.7 national percentile point gain for voucher students. For African Americans, however, the three city average gain was 6.6 percentile points, and in New York City, the black gain was 9.2 percentile points. Nonblacks saw a three city average drop of 3.5 percentile points.[4] The authors note their results are consistent with other research finding that urban minority students do disproportionately better in Catholic schools than others.[5] Howell and Peterson say the voucher test score gain for blacks is comparable to gains from reduced class size in Tennessee and larger than gains from accountability programs adopted in Texas and North Carolina.[6] Howell and Peterson argue that the results suggest programs should be expanded to include much larger numbers of students in central city urban areas.[7]

Why Do Achievement Gains Appear—and Why Only for African Americans?

The Howell and Peterson studies have been criticized on methodological grounds: critics note that a substantial number of lottery winners did not use the vouchers because they could not afford the required co-payment; the voucher programs have fairly high attrition rates; and the authors' decision to aggregate data from various grades may provide a misleading indication of the programs' effects.[8] But even assuming that the findings are completely valid, is the major policy implication they derive—expanding vouchers to more urban students—wise? To help answer that question, it is first important to know *why* vouchers produced achievement gains and why *only African Americans benefited.*

For many years there has been a running argument as to why comparable students sometimes do better in private schools than in public schools. Voucher advocates tend to believe there is something inherent in private and religious schools that offers an advantage over public schools—for example, less bureaucracy and politics or the educational benefits of a cohesive religious community. [9] Voucher opponents, by contrast, tend to believe that any observed student gains may largely be attributable to the fact that private schools provide an environment where peers and parents in the school community are self-selected and particularly motivated.[10] Classmates in private schools (or in affluent public schools) are more likely to be high achieving and academically engaged, and less likely to cause disruption; parents are more likely to be active in the school and to volunteer in class and make donations; and good teachers, all other things being equal, are more likely to be attracted to schools with highly motivated students and active parents.[11] This argument over why gains occur has crucial policy implications because if it's the demographic input (peers and parents) not the inherent structure of private schools that explains the private school advantage, voucher programs may not be successful on a broader scale. As the Rand researchers noted, if "voucher students benefited only because the program put them in classrooms with high-achieving peers, then the effect might disappear in a larger-scale program that puts large numbers of low-achieving students in voucher classrooms together."[12]

Which factor provides the more important explanation: private school policy or peers and parents? Rand's review of studies says we don't fully know the answer to this question.[13] Howell and Peterson's study is also tentative in its explanations, but it clearly doesn't rule out the peers and parents hypothesis. The authors did try to control for self-selection of *individual* students, by comparing among the winners and losers who applied for the voucher lottery, but they didn't control for the *school-level* motivation—the fact that motivated students who won the lottery were surrounded by peers and parents who are also motivated, while motivated students who lost the lottery were surrounded by the least motivated peers and parents.

Moreover, Howell and Peterson's central finding—voucher schools benefit black students, but not others—provides important new evidence that it's peers and parents, not something distinctive about private schools *per se*, that are driving achievement gains. If it were reduced bureaucracy and the distinct religious environment found in most voucher schools that makes a big difference for students, then presumably attending a voucher school would help students of *all* races. But if school quality is driven largely by peers and parents, then it's likely to particularly help those who are switching out of public schools that have less active parents and negative peer influences—specifically, high poverty public schools.[14] Who attends such schools? The research is very clear that in the United States, low-income African Americans are much more likely to attend high poverty schools than are low-income whites. While one in twenty poor whites lives in a high poverty neighborhood (more than 40 percent poor), one in three poor blacks does.[15]

Howell and Peterson don't connect the dots directly in this way themselves, but their new book is full of support for the hypothesis that voucher gains for African Americans are driven by the people who make up voucher school communities more than anything in particular about the distinctive nature of private schools *per se*.

- ***Economic Segregation by Race.*** Howell and Peterson emphasize that African Americans attend schools that are highly segregated by race and class, and therefore have more to gain from moving to voucher schools than do other poor Americans.[16] They note further that in the national privately funded voucher program they study, African Americans in segregated schools are much more likely to apply than those in less segregated schools.[17] And the authors also note that other researchers have found that the gains among blacks attending Catholic school are more than twice as large for blacks living in big cities, where poverty is most concentrated, than for other blacks.[18]

- ***Peers.*** Howell and Peterson acknowledge that leaving poverty concentrated public schools to attend private schools with more affluent classmates surely provides students with a more motivated and high achieving peer group. This is true in part because non-voucher students attending private school and paying full tuition are more advantaged than the typical public school student in a low-income school; and because low-income classmates who are self-selected voucher students provide a comparatively positive peer group.[19] While Howell and Peterson don't provide a detailed breakdown of the differences between students who applied for vouchers and those who didn't in the three cities they studied, they do outline data on those who apply to the national Child Scholarship Fund, which provides 40,000 privately funded school vouchers annually. All families need to be low income to qualify, but choosers differ in important respects from nonchoosers: they are more likely to be stable (children stayed in the same school) than those who didn't apply; and they are far more religious, with 66 percent attending church once a week, compared with 38 percent in the eligible public school pool.[20] Likewise, in San Antonio, Texas, the authors find, the baseline test scores of choosers was higher in math and considerably higher in reading than among nonchoosers.[21] The authors acknowledge that these differences can have an effect and cite a study by Caroline Hoxby finding that a one percentage point increase in classmates' test scores translates into a rise in a student's own scores of between 0.15 and 0.4 points.[22] The motivation of classmates also may have a lot to do with Howell and Peterson's finding that voucher parents report only half as often as their public school counterparts that fighting is a serious problem in the school their child attends.[23]

- **Parents.** Parental involvement has long been associated with school quality and there is strong evidence that voucher schools benefit from parental "creaming." Howell and Peterson note that families in all three cities had to provide some of their own money to participate in the voucher program, and the parents in each of these cities were much more active in the school than the parents of nonchoosers.[24]

- **Teachers.** Howell and Peterson acknowledge the possibility that teachers might have been more highly qualified in the voucher schools than in the urban public schools that students were leaving.[25] In theory, teacher quality should benefit students of all racial groups equally, but it makes sense that having adequate teachers would benefit black students in particular because strong evidence suggests that students attending economically and racially segregated public schools have far weaker teachers than students attending more affluent schools.[26]

Policy Implications

If the analysis of the data above is correct, then three policy implications seem logical.

1. ***Can't Take Vouchers to Scale.*** If we expanded the programs, as Howell and Peterson urge, to include large numbers of low-income kids, throwing the programs wide open so that private schools essentially take in the population now served by high poverty public schools, then the academic benefits the authors found are likely to be lost.[27] Once voucher schools take in large numbers of low-income students, rather than a self-selected group of students whose parents cared enough to put money down, the schools are likely to face all the difficulties of high poverty public schools—negative peer influences, low parental involvement, and less ability to attract qualified teaching staffs.

2. ***Existing Small-Scale Programs Benefit Some but Hurt Others.*** On the surface, it might appear that if it is unwise to expand voucher programs in size, small-scale programs should be implemented in additional cities so at least small numbers of African American students could benefit as they did in New York, Dayton, and Washington. But this analysis ignores the impact of vouchers on the much larger number of students who remain in public schools. Howell and Peterson's research suggests students stuck in public schools (including the control group) do not perform very well. Moreover, if the reason self-selected African American students do better in voucher schools is that they are leaving negative school environments associated with concentrated poverty, the huge numbers of children left behind may be marginally *worse off*, because some of the most motivated low-income peers and parents have left.[28]

   Howell and Peterson try to address this concern by arguing that even though the public school students left behind enjoy a less favorable peer and parent–school community, they may benefit because voucher programs place competitive pressures on public schools to improve. But the authors concede that this research is disputed and themselves provide no new data on this crucial question.[29] In any event, if the creaming issue is a powerful negative force on students left behind in public schools, wouldn't it make more sense to find ways to garner the competitive benefits of choice, without incurring the strong inequities associated with peer stratification?

3. **ANOTHER ALTERNATIVE: WIDESPREAD PUBLIC SCHOOL CHOICE.** Is there a way to avoid the Catch 22 of voucher programs—that if they stay small, they leave most students behind and worse off, but if they are expanded, they lose their effectiveness? Is there a way to respond to the compelling argument of choice supporters—that the current system unfairly rations educational opportunity through the housing market—in a manner that helps *all* low-income students, not just a few? A way to provide a diversity of school offerings and the potential competitive pressures provided by choice without further stratifying students?

   If the limited size of voucher programs means they can't be taken to scale, there is another alternative that can be: widespread public school choice. Instead of trying a large-scale voucher experiment that is destined to fail, we should encourage a large-scale public school choice program that is likely to succeed.

Middle class public schools, like private schools, have relatively good teachers, manageable discipline problems, motivated peers, active parents and high expectations that can benefit all children who attend such schools, middle class and low income. As Howell and Peterson themselves note, significant achievement gains were found among low-income students who attended middle class public schools using a housing voucher under the federal Moving to Opportunities program (compared with equally motivated low-income students who lost the lottery and remained in high poverty public schools.)[30]

Instead of trying to pack low-income kids into a tiny number of private voucher schools, public school choice programs can build on the success of thousands of middle class public schools. Nationally, about two-thirds of public school students are middle class (not eligible for free and reduced price lunch). Bringing all public schools into a system of choice would potentially allow every child to attend a solidly middle class public school. Studies suggest that low-income achievement will rise, and middle class achievement will not suffer so long as schools are more than 50 percent middle class.[31]

Public school choice systems, like vouchers, can be subject to creaming, so it is important that programs be structured carefully. The trick is to make choice work to promote, rather than undercut, equality of opportunity, educational achievement, and social cohesion. Successful public school choice systems have three ingredients.

- *FIRST, CHOICE SHOULD BE MANDATORY.* Cambridge, Massachusetts, and that a number of other jurisdictions have eliminated the old system that assigns students based on where their parents can afford to live and instead requires every parent to choose from a variety of options. Self-selection is avoided, the Rand study notes, because where all students are required to choose, "the problem of non-choosers disappear."[32] Every school is magnetized based on community sentiment about the types of pedagogical and thematic offerings that are desired. Public schools compete for parents. Under-chosen schools can be closed down or redesigned, and over-chosen schools can be franchised.

- *SECOND, CHOICE PLANS SHOULD BE SUBJECT TO FAIRNESS GUIDELINES.* While Americans are strongly opposed to busing, they are supportive of fairness guidelines to help ensure that public school choice promotes integration.[33] In a number of communities, from Cambridge to Raleigh, North Carolina, from San Francisco to La Crosse, Wisconsin, communities have adopted guidelines to ensure that all schools have a strong core of middle class families.[34]

- *THIRD, TO BE SUCCESSFUL, PUBLIC SCHOOL CHOICE SHOULD BE ALLOWED ACROSS SCHOOL DISTRICT LINES, FOLLOWING SUCCESSFUL MODELS IN ST. LOUIS, HARTFORD, AND BOSTON*. While some might think the prospect of interdistrict choice is politically unfeasible, polls find 75 percent of Americans support such interdistrict public school choice.[35] Today, 300,000 students attend public schools of choice across district lines—twenty times the number that participate in publicly funded private school vouchers programs (see Figure 3.1).

The new federal education legislation, the No Child Left Behind Act, moves us in the direction of public school choice for economic and academic integration. The act requires all districts to provide public school choice for children trapped in failing schools to attend better performing public schools. This legislation, which requires a form of desegregation by student achievement, also requires that low-income students be given priority when space is limited, a tacit endorsement of the importance of economic integration.

The idea behind public school choice is to combine the best elements of vouchers while avoiding their downside. By moving beyond a system of assignment that ties school quality to the value of housing, public school choice can make the important strides toward equity that choice advocates say they want. Public school choice also allows students to better fit their learning needs by offering a Montessori program at one school, or a concentration on computers at another. Howell and Peterson acknowledge that such public school choice mechanisms, like magnet schools, have been associated with test score gains, even after addressing self-selection issues.[36] Whatever benefits stem from competition between schools are also likely to be had with public school choice. But at the same time, the various difficulties and dangers associated with vouchers—issues of creaming, and Balkanization—can be avoided by folding choice into the existing system of public schooling that has served our democracy so well for so many years.

4.

Myth #2: Vouchers Are Part of the New Civil Rights Movement

Vouchers and *Brown v. Board of Education*

Richard C. Leone

In 2002, the national debate about education has been focused on the issues related to the use of public money to support private and religious education. Would schools work better if parents "shopped" for them as consumers? Or, does the premise that the state has a responsibility to educate future citizens still hold true? The June Supreme Court decision in the Cleveland voucher case potentially cleared the way for struggles throughout the nation between opponents and advocates of such private funding mechanisms. Somewhat astonishingly, the president went so far as to liken the Court's decision as similar in importance to the landmark *Brown v. Board of Education* decision ending school segregation in the South. Education secretary Rod Paige went further to suggest that vouchers are part of "a new civil rights revolution" that could help liberate blacks along the lines of the *Brown* ruling. But for those who must grapple with the mission of improving education in those school systems with serious problems, it is not clear that these cases are similar.

The unequal character of elementary and secondary educational opportunity in the nation is scarcely likely to be redressed by the Court

---

Excerpts from *Divided We Fail: Coming Together through Public School Choice: The Report of The Century Foundation Task Force on the Common School* (New York: Century Foundation Press, 2002).

decision or by the generally modest grants (vouchers) envisioned to underwrite nonpublic schools. If our nation is serious about reinventing the goals of *Brown* for the twenty-first century, we will need to think a great deal more imaginatively than the simplistic notions of privatization and competition that underpin support for vouchers.

In the first place, the "promise" of vouchers is premised on the notion that they eventually will be used by a great many American elementary and secondary schoolchildren. As of this writing, however, vouchers are available to only one-tenth of one percent of public school students and therefore are a negligible factor in education policy (although they obviously have a disproportionate effect on the political debate). Many questions about the potential for voucher systems to grow dramatically are, at this point, unanswered, particularly those relating to how vouchers could be expanded to a scale that was significant. Moreover, if, as many fear, vouchers wind up "creaming" the best students and most discriminating parents away from public schools, is it possible that their expansion will actually take us further away from the goals of *Brown*?

So far, experience with voucher programs hardly supports the comparison to *Brown*. In fact, in the years following that 1954 decision, private school vouchers were used as a means to circumvent desegregation. Most voucher schemes today make no conscious efforts to promote integration, and experience from other countries suggests vouchers will lead to more stratification by class and race, not less. In other words, despite the recent Court decision and the claims of voucher advocates, it is still reasonable to assume that the large-scale solutions to American education issues—if they are to come at all—will come within the framework of public school systems. And, that was the wise premise adopted by this Task Force.

The members of the Task Force accept the legitimate premise of voucher supporters—that it is unfair to trap poor children in failing schools—but recognize that large-scale solutions to America's education issues will come from providing choice within the public school system, where 90 percent of American children are educated and where public policy measures can help ensure that choice promotes equal opportunity. At a time when our nation is more diverse than ever before, when education is more important than ever before, and public education is under attack as never before, the Task Force sets out a timely blueprint for restoring the American common school.

Vouchers and Segregation

The Century Foundation Task Force
on the Common School

The Task Force strongly believes that school choice should take place within the public school system. If the goal is economically and racially integrated schools that will promote equal opportunity and social cohesion, private school vouchers take us in precisely the wrong direction. Three features fundamentally distinguish private schools from public schools—their selectivity; their appeal to niche markets; and their independent nature—and each undermines the goals we seek to promote.

While public schools generally take all comers, private schools pride themselves on the ability to select students for admissions.[1] Therefore, private school choice plans normally give the final choice to schools, not to parents. And where private schools are required by law to admit students by lottery, the number of schools willing to participate is severely limited.[2] Private schools normally select for admission more affluent students, not because they have an animus against lower income students, but because more privileged students are on average easier to teach. Voucher-type plans in Sweden, Chile, New Zealand, and the Netherlands have all increased social stratification.[3]

Private schools also are designed by their very nature to "segment" the market, emphasizing difference rather than commonality. Most emphasize religious differences—some 84.3 percent of American students attending private schools attend religious schools[4]—and some emphasize differences by nationality or race. As the late Albert Shanker of the American Federation of Teachers noted, with vouchers "you'll end up with kids of different religions, nationalities and languages going

---

Excerpts from *Divided We Fail: Coming Together through Public School Choice: The Report of The Century Foundation Task Force on the Common School* (New York: Century Foundation Press, 2002).

off to different schools to maintain their separateness and I think we'd have a terrible social price to pay for it."[5]

Finally, private schools are, by their nature, "independent" schools—independent of democratically elected officials. Private schools cannot be required to teach democratic principles, or values such as tolerance; and even when they receive public funding, they are not bound by the U.S. Constitution. Though President George W. Bush places testing and accountability at the center of his effort to improve public schools, his plan for private school vouchers did not call for any testing of students.[6]

Choice and Segregation in New Zealand

Edward B. Fiske and Helen F. Ladd

Some of the most widely discussed and controversial proposals for reforming American schools focus on the twin themes of giving local schools more operational autonomy and forcing them to compete for students. Proponents of charter schools and voucher plans argue that schools must be liberated from the controlling hands of educational bureaucrats. If such operational freedom is combined with parental choice, the argument goes, both the means and the incentives will be in place for schools to deliver quality teaching and learning.

Domestic evidence that would confirm or discredit this proposition is scarce. The charter school movement in the United States is too recent and current voucher experiments too small to shed any light on the likely consequences of bringing them to scale. What policy makers need is evidence from a large-scale and long-term experiment with self-governing schools operating in a competitive environment.

Fortunately, such evidence exists. In 1989, New Zealand, under a Labour government, abolished its long-standing, and bureaucratically stifling, centralized system of school governance and turned operational control of each of the country's 2,700 primary and secondary schools over to locally elected boards of trustees dominated by parents. Two years later, a newly elected national government, pursuing an aggressive New Right agenda, ratcheted the reform stakes up a notch by abolishing enrollment zones and giving parents the right to seek to enroll their child in any public school. These changes persist to this day.

Originally published as "The Invisible Hand as Schoolmaster." Reprinted with permission from *The American Prospect* Volume 11, Number 13: May 22, 2000. *The American Prospect*, 5 Broad Street, Boston, MA 02109.

New Zealand's experience with what were collectively known as the Tomorrow's Schools reforms has direct relevance to the school reform debate in this country. With 3.8 million citizens, New Zealand has the same population as that of the median American state, and its Ministry of Education is thus the functional equivalent of a state education department under our decentralized system. New Zealand has similar social, cultural, and political traditions, and, perhaps most importantly, it has a significant minority population, with Maori making up 14 percent of the total and Pacific Islanders another 6 percent. The urgent educational and other problems faced by urban Maori in Alan Duff's wrenching book and the subsequent movie *Once Were Warriors* offer striking parallels to the situation in our own inner cities.

During five months in early 1998, we had the opportunity to assess the impact of the Tomorrow's Schools reforms in urban areas through visits to nearly 50 schools, analysis of government data, and interviews with political and educational leaders at the national and local levels. We believe that New Zealand's ambitious and bold reforms provide a number of powerful insights for the U.S. debate.

It is important to note at the outset that schools in New Zealand are generally happy with their new self-governing status, and virtually no one wants to go back to the highly controlled system of the past, when schools could not even make unilateral decisions about the color of classroom walls. Parental choice has also been hugely appealing, and it has had a profound impact on enrollment patterns.

One tool for measuring the magnitude and nature of enrollment changes is New Zealand's system of assigning decile rankings to schools based on the socioeconomic and ethnic characteristics of the students they attract. These deciles were developed so that supplementary funding could be distributed to the schools with the most challenging-to-educate students. Low-decile schools serve large proportions of minority children and students from disadvantaged backgrounds. Students in high-decile schools tend to come from predominantly affluent and European families.

Research by us and others shows that, in the minds of New Zealand parents seeking to evaluate schools, a high-decile ranking—and hence an attractive mix of students—is a proxy for academic quality. As a result, since the advent of choice in 1991, there has been a distinct upward shift in enrollment, with low-decile schools facing declining rolls and high-decile schools growing in size.

To deal with oversubscribed schools, New Zealand allows any school with more applicants than places available to draft an "enrollment scheme" spelling out the criteria it will use for selecting students. Because such schools have become increasingly common over time—by 1997 over 50 percent of urban secondary-school students were in schools that had enrollment schemes—the system has effectively shifted from parental choice to one in which schools do the choosing.

Because New Zealand does not carry out systematic national testing, we cannot determine whether the combination of self-governing schools in a competitive environment has increased average student achievement. It seems fair to surmise, though, that teaching and learning may well have improved at the high end of the scale, where schools with enrollment schemes can handpick students and target teaching to them.

Although New Zealanders clearly enjoy the empowerment of self-governance and parental choice in their state school system, the new system has generated some serious concerns that policy makers are now being forced to address.

First, the combination of self-governing schools in a competitive environment has increased ethnic polarization of the state education system. Although both European and minority families have participated in the movement from low- to high-decile schools, the former have been more aggressive in taking advantage of the choice option than have Maori or Pacific Islanders. Thus, ethnic minorities have become increasingly concentrated in low-decile schools.

Between 1991 and 1996, for example, the share of minorities in decile 1 primary and intermediate schools in the capital city of Wellington rose from 76 to 82 percent—a shift that cannot be explained by changes in ethnic residential patterns as measured by census data. At the secondary level, even greater changes occurred, although the patterns were a bit more complex as some minorities moved from decile 1 to decile 2 schools while Europeans fled from both. The net effect was a large increase in the proportion of minorities in the low-decile schools. Piecemeal evidence from a ministry-financed study indicates that school enrollments have also become more segregated socioeconomically.

From the point of view of parents, moving up the decile scale in choice of school is understandable and even rational. Higher-decile schools are likely to attract higher-quality teachers, and their mix of students could well generate positive spillover effects on student motivation. The result, however, is that schools with a large percentage of minorities are at a competitive disadvantage in the marketplace in attracting students. Moreover, evidence shows that the terms of enrollment schemes and the cost of transportation have limited the access of minority students to the upper-decile schools.

One can reasonably ask whether the increased ethnic and socioeconomic polarization is a problem. We believe it is. The Hippocratic oath taken by new physicians begins with the declaration "First do no harm." While state school systems cannot be expected to solve all social problems, they should at a minimum not exacerbate existing inequities. Ideally, they should serve to offset them. Although other countries might design a competitive system somewhat different from New Zealand's, the forces unleashed by parental choice, including the use of student mix as a proxy for academic quality, are likely to push systems toward greater ethnic and socioeconomic polarization under any circumstances.

A second concern has to do with winners and losers. By definition, in any competitive environment some participants will be successful, and others will fail. That's the way markets work. We observed situations in New Zealand where two schools operating on a level playing field were engaged in vigorous competition for students, which probably redounded to the benefit of both. In a comfortable suburb of Wellington, for example, Heretaunga College has increased its enrollment at the expense of nearby Upper Hutt College. Both are viable high schools, though, and the competition appears to have energized them both.

The problem is that the playing field is not always level. Difficult-to-teach students—those from poverty-stricken homes, those whose English is weak, those with learning difficulties—are concentrated in schools at the bottom. Statistics on students who are suspended for disciplinary reasons show that they are far more likely to move down the decile ladder than up. The result is a widening of the gap between the low- and high-decile schools in terms of the mix of students they serve and their average test scores on school exit exams.

New Zealanders describe the loser schools as "spiraling" downward. Once they begin to fall behind in the educational marketplace, downward spiraling schools find their problems compounding and feeding on each other. Lower student rolls mean fewer teachers, which mean a less attractive academic program, which means even fewer students. Schools become losers; so do the students and families served by them.

The question thus arises whether it is defensible—on moral, practical, or other grounds—to organize the delivery of public education so that it is clear from the outset that, when the system is working properly, the problems of some schools will be seriously exacerbated.

Two conditions might justify such a policy. First, if competition led to an overall improvement of the system as a whole, the losers would still be winners in absolute terms. The second condition would be realized if the Ministry of Education, aware that competition leads inevitably to unsuccessful schools, stood ready with a safety net to provide assistance once schools began to fail. Neither condition, however, was present in New Zealand.

Our third concern relates to the balancing of legitimate but competing interests. Any state educational system has a multitude of stakeholders, from students and parents to employers and the body politic. The original Tomorrow's Schools reform plan called for a number of mechanisms to balance these interests, including the creation of community forums to deal with local conflicts and the use of lotteries to decide which students would be admitted to oversubscribed schools. Largely for political reasons, however, these mechanisms fell by the wayside.

Instead, primacy was given to the rights of current parents in a particular school. Thus, when the boards of several primary schools decided to add two more grades so their parents would not have to send their children to the local intermediate school—decisions with significant consequences for other schools and parents in their areas—they were free to pursue their own self-interest. The new system also showed its faith in the capacity of an educational marketplace to balance competing interests by giving oversubscribed schools the right to accept and reject students with little reference to how their decisions would affect other schools or the system as a whole.

Over the years, as the consequences of this laissez-faire approach became clear, the Ministry of Education was forced to make some changes. Primary schools no longer have carte blanche to add grades, and new regulations guarantee access to "a reasonably convenient school."

Perhaps most importantly, political embarrassment over spiraling schools has forced the ministry to intervene directly to assist troubled inner-city schools even though there is nothing in the theory of self-governing schools in a competitive environment that would justify such intervention. Rather than attempting to reconcile theory with the plight of spiraling schools, Ministry officials have simply conceded that such a system simply will not work for 10 to 20 percent of schools. Specifically, they have acknowledged that autonomy and choice cannot, in and of themselves, meet the challenges of troubled urban schools.

Are the results from New Zealand inevitable? Not fully. In retrospect, it is clear that different policy decisions could have been made. The United States and other countries need not follow New Zealand's lead in giving schools control over enrollment schemes, for instance. Nevertheless, given family concern about the mix of students, there is likely to be intense pressure for ethnic polarization in any system of parental choice.

Any market-based system is also likely to create losers unless the government takes explicit action to improve teaching and learning in those schools. It is noteworthy that low-decile schools had operational autonomy, strong incentives to improve the quality of their offerings, some good managers, and, under a progressive funding system, more funding per pupil than high-decile ones. Still, they were unable to compete successfully

The clear conclusion is that school autonomy and strong incentives to attract students are not sufficient to overcome the serious challenges faced by schools with disproportionate shares of low-performing students. Policies are needed that address more directly the challenges of teaching and learning in such schools.

Institutions or procedures also can be introduced to balance competing interests. One example is the "controlled choice" plans in Cambridge, Massachusetts, where parents list their preferences for particular schools, but assignments are made centrally with an eye toward balancing the racial makeup of schools and other factors. A system of "contract schools" could potentially provide another model. The point is that explicit attention to the balancing of interests of various stakeholders is needed. The invisible hand does not work.

The architects of Tomorrow's Schools put their faith in simple governance solutions to complex questions of educational quality, and they found them wanting. Any country that seeks to follow New Zealand's lead would do well to understand the limitations of market-based reforms and to build in appropriate safeguards from the start.

Private Schools and Segregation

Sean F. Reardon and John T. Yun

For the last half century there has been intensive focus on the racial segregation of public schools in the United States. Extensive research on public school enrollments has shown that public school integration increased substantially under the enforcement of civil rights laws in the late 1960s and 1970s but has undergone a slow but steady decline since the late 1980s. There has, however, been a curious lack of information about, and interest in, the racial enrollment patterns of the nation's private school students, over eighty percent of whom attend religious schools. Examination of private school racial enrollment patterns is particularly important now, given 1) the increasing diversity of the United States; 2) the fact that there are few white students enrolled in the public schools of many central cities; 3) the fact that private school enrollments are on the rise; and 4) current efforts to legalize public aid for religious schools through voucher programs—efforts that are based in part on claims about the superiority of private education.

This report describes recent patterns of racial enrollments in private K–12 schools in the United States. There has never been a major report on private school segregation based on comprehensive national data. Instead, much of the discussion about private school racial enrollment patterns is based on relatively small samples of private schools in national studies, samples that cannot be reliably used to project national or sub-national patterns. This report is possible because the federal government initiated a Private School Survey in 1993, providing comprehensive national data with an extremely high response rate from

---

Executive Summary from "Private School Racial Enrollments and Segregation," Civil Rights Project, Harvard University, Cambridge, Massachusetts, 2002. Reprinted with permission of The President and Fellows of Harvard College.

the nation's private schools. This report includes data from the most recently available survey, which covers the 1997–98 school year.

Segregation Patterns

The most significant finding in this report is that segregation levels are quite high among private schools, particularly among Catholic and other religious private schools, where the levels of segregation are often equal or greater than levels of segregation among public schools. In particular, we highlight the following results.

- Black–white segregation is greater among private schools than among public schools. Although 78 percent of the private school students in the nation were white in 1997–98, the average black private school student was enrolled in a school that was only 34 percent white. For comparison, note that among public schools, 64 percent of students were white and the average black public school student attended a school that was 33 percent white. In other words, black private school students are as racially isolated as black public school students. Despite the fact that black students constitute a much smaller share of the private school population than the public school population, black and white private school students largely attend separate schools.

- Black–white segregation is greatest among Catholic schools. Black Catholic school students attend schools that are, on average, 31 percent white; black students in non-Catholic religious schools attend schools that average 35 percent white; and black students in secular private schools attend schools that average 41 percent white. Secular private schools are considerably less segregated than public schools.

- In both the South and the West—where white students make up a much smaller share of the population than elsewhere, and where black–white public school segregation is the lowest in the country—private schools are much more segregated than their public school counterparts. In the South, black students attend private schools that are, on average, 39 percent white and public schools that are 36 percent white. Given that 80 percent of private and 58 percent of public school students in the South are white, the similar levels of exposure to whites in schools indicate that private schools are far more segregated than public schools. Similarly, in the West, where 65 percent of private and 52 percent of public school students are white, black students attend private schools that average 35 percent white and public schools that average 32 percent white, again indicating higher levels of private than public segregation.

- Black–white private school segregation is much greater among private schools in large metropolitan areas than in smaller metropolitan areas and rural areas.

- Latino–white segregation is lower among private schools than among public schools. Although 78 percent of the private school students in the nation were white in 1997–98, the average Latino private school student was enrolled in a school that was only 41 percent white. For comparison, note that among public schools, 64 percent of students were white, and the average Latino public school student attended a school that was only 30 percent white. Latino public school students are thus more racially isolated than black public school students, but Latino private school students are more racially integrated than black private school students.

- Latino–white segregation is greatest among public and Catholic schools. Latino Catholic school students attend schools that are, on average, 36 percent white; Latino students in non-Catholic religious schools attend schools that average 51 percent white; and Latino students in secular private schools attend schools that average 50 percent white. Non-Catholic religious schools and secular private schools are considerably less segregated than public and Catholic schools for Latino students. Catholic schools enroll over two-thirds of Latino private school students, so segregation levels among Catholic schools are the most significant for Latino students.

- White students are more racially isolated in private schools than in public schools. In public schools 47 percent of white students attend schools that are 90–100 percent white, while in private schools 64 percent of white students attend schools that are 90–100 percent white. In private schools, white students attend schools that are, on average, almost nine-tenths (88 percent) white and only 12 percent minority, whereas white students in public schools attend schools that average four-fifths (81 percent) white and one-fifth (19 percent) minority.

- White students are most isolated in Catholic and other religious private schools. The racial isolation of white students is greatest in non-Catholic religious schools, where the average white student attends a school that is 90 percent white and where 69 percent of white students attend schools that are 90–100 percent white. White students are only slightly less isolated in Catholic schools, where the average white student attends a school that is 89 percent white and where 66 percent of white students attend schools that are 90–100 percent white. Secular private schools, in contrast, have relatively low levels of white racial isolation—white students in secular private schools attend schools that are, on average, 85 percent white, and 44 percent of white students in secular schools are in schools that are 90–100 percent white.

- Among private schools, secular private schools have the most racially diverse enrollments and the lowest levels of segregation. Non-sectarian private schools have the highest rate of minority enrollment among private schools. Catholic school enrollments are slightly less diverse, while non-Catholic religious schools enroll the least diverse population of students. Within the private sector, segregation is greatest among Catholic schools, followed by other religious schools, and lowest among secular private schools.

- Catholic and other religious schools are highly segregated in part because of residential segregation patterns. The high level of segregation among Catholic schools is largely due to the fact that most Catholic schools draw their enrollments from local, highly segregated, neighborhoods. Absent any systematic mandate and effort to create integrated schools, Catholic school enrollment patterns typically mirror segregated residential patterns, often to a greater extent than in public schools, where desegregation efforts have often achieved some level of racial integration. In contrast, the relatively lower levels of racial isolation and segregation among secular private schools may be due to the fact that many of these schools draw students from a broad geographic area and, in many cases, actively seek to attract and retain a diverse student population.

ENROLLMENT

Private schools are still a small sector of the nation's schools, enrolling roughly one-tenth of the K–12 students in the United States. Private sector enrollments have been relatively stable since the early 1970s, though they appear to have increased slowly during the 1990s. Within the relatively constant share of private school students, Catholic schools have been in a long decline but are still dominant, enrolling roughly half of all private school students in the late 1990s. Other religious private schools—often evangelical Christian schools—have been increasing their share of private schools the most rapidly and now enroll roughly one-third of all private school students. Secular private schools enroll the remaining one-sixth of private school students.

Patterns of private school enrollment vary considerably across the country and among different segments of the population. In particular, localized racial and socioeconomic differences in private school enrollment rates are important because they may create substantial patterns of segregation between the public and private sectors. This report describes these patterns in detail; several key findings are below.

- White and Asian students enroll in private schools at two times the rate of black and Latino students. Nationally, 12 percent of white students and 11 percent of Asian students are enrolled in private schools, while only 5 percent of black and 6 percent of Latino students are enrolled in private schools. Nonetheless, despite the racial differences in private school enrollment, nationwide, 88 percent to 96 percent of students of all racial groups attend public schools.

- Private school enrollment rates are much higher among middle- and high-income families than low-income families. As expected, private school enrollment rates rise consistently with income, with about one in 25 low-income students (those with family incomes below $20,000/year) enrolled in private school compared to about one in six upper-income students (those from families earning $50,000/year or more). Almost two-thirds of students in private schools (63 percent) are from families with incomes greater than $50,000; less than 40 percent of students in public schools are from similar families. Likewise, only 8 percent of private school students are from families with incomes below $20,000, compared to over 22 percent of public school students.

- At all income levels, white private school enrollment rates are greater than black and Latino private school enrollment rates. Differences in private school enrollment rates cannot be explained as a result of income differences alone. At every income level, white students are more likely to be in private schools than are black and Latino students. The combination of income and racial enrollment patterns means that middle- and upper middle-class white students are substantially over-represented in private schools. In fact, over half (53 percent) of all private school students in 1998–2000 were non-Hispanic white students from families with annual incomes over $50,000. The comparable figure in public schools was 32 percent.

- Differences in white and minority private school enrollment rates contribute substantially to overall patterns of segregation in many local school markets. Although white private school enrollments are twice minority private school enrollments nationally, in many local schooling markets, white and minority private school enrollment differences can be much higher, between 3-10 times larger, resulting in substantial segregation between the public and private sectors.

- In large school districts, stark differences between white and minority school enrollment rates result in high levels of segregation between public and private schools. In the 40 largest school districts in the United States—most of which are large urban school districts or large county-wide school districts in the South, and that collectively contain over 7 million students, one-third of whom are black students—31 percent of white students attend private schools, compared to 10 percent of black and 12 percent of Latino students living in these same districts. As a result, the public schools in these districts have a student population that is 33 percent white, while the private school population of these districts is 63 percent white, a difference of 30 percentage points.

- On average, white private school enrollment rates are highest in school districts with large proportions of black students in the population. A plot showing white private school enrollment rates by district proportion black shows a strong positive trend, suggesting that some white families may use the private sector as a way of ensuring that their children attend schools with greater proportions of white students than may be available in the public sector.

- In many large school districts, more than one-third of all white students living within the district are enrolled in private schools. A number of large urban districts lose much of their white student population to private schools. The large school districts with the highest white private school enrollment rates are generally the large urban districts of the Northeast and Midwest. The districts with the highest white private school enrollment rates in 1989–90 were Washington, DC (67 percent), New Orleans (65 percent), Philadelphia (55 percent), Chicago (54 percent), Jefferson Parish, LA (50 percent), San Francisco (49 percent), Boston (48 percent), Cleveland (47 percent), New York City (45 percent), and Milwaukee (41 percent).

Implications

From a civil rights perspective, several key points emerge from this report. First, the assumption that private schools enroll the greatest percentage of students in the South, where there has been the highest level of public school integration and by far the highest proportion of black students in the population, is simply wrong. Although the South has by far the highest proportion of black students in the public schools whites attend, it has a relatively small private school sector, just 8 percent, as does the West where almost half of the public school students are nonwhite. Moreover, white private school enrollment rates in the South (11 percent) are lower than the U.S. average (12 percent), suggesting that there is not (or no longer) any substantial "white flight" to private schools in the South to avoid integrated public school systems. No southern or western state except Louisiana (a historic center of Catholic settlement) was among the 15 states with the highest share of students in private schools. Among metropolitan areas, New Orleans and New York had by far the highest share of white students in private schools.

Second, the assumption that minority students experience higher levels of integration with whites in the private sector when compared to the public sector is simply not true, particularly for black students. The discussion about vouchers has often included claims that minority students would get access to schools like whites—a similar set of choices—if only they had greater access to the private sector. In fact, black students in the private sector are just as segregated from whites as in the public sector; white students in the private sector generally attend overwhelmingly white schools. In addition, while Latino private school students make up only a small fraction of private school enrollments, they still experience schools that typically have substantial non-white majorities. Since private schools typically provide no free transportation for students, an increase in the minority percentages in these schools would be likely to increase segregation.

Third, the data presented here suggest that a number of frequent generalizations about public and private education in the United States are not accurate. In particular, the data indicate that, in spite of local variations, private schools provide education for only a small minority of American students. The fact that the large metropolitan areas—including the New York and Los Angeles metropolitan areas, which dominate the nation's media—have among the highest proportions of white students in private schools may well account for the inaccurate perception that public schools are threatened by private school growth.

Fourth, this report suggests several interesting things about the theory that desegregation produces white flight to private schools. On the one hand, much of this research shows little evidence of white flight from desegregation. For example, private schools enroll the most students in regions (the Northeast and Midwest) where public schools enroll the fewest minorities, and the fewest in the regions (the South and West) where the most interracial contact in public schools takes place. In addition, white private school enrollment rates peaked from 1950–1965, before there was any significant attempt at desegregation; then, after declining sharply in the late 1960s, white private school enrollments were relatively stable through the 1970s, the period of greatest desegregation. Moreover, in the last decade, as segregation has increased among public schools, white private school enrollment rates have increased gradually. Although many other factors contribute to these trends—including national declines in Catholic school enrollments, economic cycles, tuition trends, and perceptions of public school quality—these trends are nonetheless exactly the opposite of what white flight from desegregation would be expected to produce.

On the other hand, some of the evidence suggests that some whites may seek private schooling in part to avoid schools with large minority enrollments. In school districts and metropolitan areas with higher shares of black students in the population, a higher proportion of whites attend private schools. In many large districts and in many metropolitan areas with high proportions of black students, white students are enrolled in private schools at rates far greater than black and Latino students. Moreover, it appears that this pattern cannot be attributed to white avoidance of public schools where poverty rates are high, since the strong association between white private enrollments and black student populations persists after we take local poverty rates into account. In all of our models, the strongest predictor of white private enrollment is the proportion of black students in the area.

Finally, it is important to note that this report cannot definitively ascertain the causes of these patterns of racial enrollment. The data do, however, suggest that private schools, as now operated, are not a significant answer to the problems caused by intensifying racial isolation in public schools as desegregation is abandoned. Other recent research from The Civil Rights Project has shown strong academic and adult life benefits of education in racially diverse schools. We recommend that the leaders of the nation's religious and secular private schools examine these patterns and the isolation of their significant minority enrollments as well as the serious segregation of white students and consider recruitment and transportation policies that could produce more diverse educational experiences for students of all racial and ethnic groups.

Charter Schools and Racial and Social Class Segregation: Yet Another Sorting Machine?

Amy Stuart Wells, Jennifer Jellison Holme, Alejandra Lopez, and Camille Wilson Cooper

One of the most troubling contradictions of our time is that, as our society becomes more racially and ethnically diverse, our public schools are becoming more racially and ethnically homogeneous. Indeed, in the past twenty years, judges and policymakers have removed many of the formal mechanisms—such as court orders and student transfer policies—designed to create more desegregated public schools.

These developments are even more paradoxical in light of recent public opinion data that show more people in the United States than ever before say they believe that public schools should be racially diverse. For example, a 1994 Gallup poll found that the percentage of the American people who said "more should be done to integrate schools" had risen rapidly, from 37 percent in 1988 to 56 percent in 1994.[1] A 1998 survey found that 80 percent of African-American parents and 66 percent of white parents surveyed said that it was either "very important" or "somewhat important" that their children's schools be racially integrated. Only 8 percent of black parents and 17 percent of white parents said less should be done to achieve racial integration in schools.[2]

Excerpts from Amy Stuart Wells et al., "Charter Schools and Racial and Social Class Segregation: Yet Another Sorting Machine?" in *A Notion at Risk: Preserving Public Education as an Engine for Social Mobility* (New York: Century Foundation Press, 2000).

At the same time, there is a growing body of research demonstrating the positive impact of school desegregation on the social mobility and life chances of African Americans. For instance, a review of the literature on the long-term effects of school desegregation found that African-American graduates of racially diverse schools had higher occupational aspirations and better understood the steps needed to obtain their goals than graduates of all-black schools. This review also noted that African-American graduates of desegregated high schools were more likely to attend predominantly white universities and earn higher degrees.[3] And finally, African Americans who had attended racially mixed schools were more likely to be working in white-collar and professional jobs in integrated corporations and institutions. They also had more integrated social and professional networks through which they learned about employment opportunities.[4]

Yet, despite opinion polls and research supporting integration, since 1988 public schools have become more racially and ethnically segregated as more districts are released from desegregation orders and urban schools become increasingly racially isolated. According to Gary Orfield and his colleagues, this shift has been most striking in the southern and border states and is most severe for Latino students—the fastest growing student population in the country.[5]

Thus, we are dismantling the mechanisms by which we desegregate public schools at the same time that the perceived need for more racially diverse schools is quite high and the positive, long-term impact of desegregation is better documented than ever before. Indeed, it seems as though this is an appropriate moment in the history of our country to question whether or not the goals of racial integration should be transferred to new educational policies. Yet to date, most policymakers remain resistant to crafting new policies, such as charter school laws, in ways that strongly support the goals of racial diversity in public schools. For instance, while virtually all thirty-six state charter school laws include anti-discrimination clauses and several give preference to schools that enroll "at-risk" students (often without defining what that means), very few laws specifically require racial or socioeconomic balance in charter schools. And even in states with laws requiring some racial balance for charter schools, there is little evidence that either state officials or local school districts are monitoring charter schools' compliance. In fact, in South Carolina—one of the states with the strictest racial balance guidelines for charter schools—a state judge recently declared these guidelines unconstitutional.[6]

Furthermore, none of the laws provide meaningful incentives such as grants or other forms of support for people to create racially diverse schools.

But it is precisely this lack of regulation and requirement that is at the heart of charter school reform—a movement that allows schools to operate with public money but less government oversight. Given the laissez-faire nature of this very popular and rapidly expanding reform, skeptics fear that it will create greater racial/ethnic and socioeconomic segregation and stratification in the way that similar deregulated school choice policies in other countries have.[7]

Yet, charter school proponents claim that theirs is not an elitist movement that enables wealthy and white families to flee the regular public schools, thereby exacerbating racial and social class segregation.[8] Far from that, they say that charter schools are serving many disadvantaged students. Some even argue that a parent's right to choose a school, including a charter school, is the new civil rights issue of our time.[9]

Furthermore, several reports have shown that charter schools do indeed serve low-income students and students of color. In fact, in some states, comparisons of statewide averages demonstrate that charter schools serve these students at a higher rate than the public schools.[10] However, these data do not speak to the issue of racial/ethnic or socioeconomic isolation within and across charter schools. In fact, there is generally very little discussion of this isolation in most of these reports (many conducted by people and/or institutions that advocate charter school reform) or how its presence—or absence—relates to different students' opportunities to learn within these schools.

Thus, beyond the fears and proclamations of skeptics and proponents are a set of important questions about who is enrolled in charter schools in different states and local communities, how they got there, and why. In this chapter, we begin to answer some of these questions by reviewing more than twenty studies of charter schools—conducted by independent researchers—so that we can begin an informed dialogue about these important issues.[11] As far as we know, this is the most comprehensive review of the literature in this area to date.

After reviewing the literature and drawing from our own study of charter schools in ten California school districts, we argue that currently there is not sufficient evidence to support strongly either the assertion that charter schools will exacerbate segregation and inequality or that they will help to overcome them. Still, we note that there is enough evidence to suggest that charter schools are less racially and socioeconomically diverse than the already segregated public schools, albeit for different reasons in different states and communities. Thus, there is cause for concern that the current charter school legislation does not promote the creation of racially and socioeconomically diverse charter schools.

In the first section of this chapter, we examine the research on who is being served in charter schools. Here we report that despite the aggregated national data that show that low-income students and students of color are enrolled in charter schools, the context of the reform—where it is being implemented and why—matters a great deal in terms of who is served. It appears that in some states charter school reform is mostly an urban phenomenon, serving predominantly low-income students of color. In other states, it appeals to a much wider range of people and communities, including many that are disproportionately white and well-off.

In fact, our analysis suggests that, in many instances, states with more racially/ethnically and socioeconomically diverse K–12 student populations tend to have charter schools that enroll a disproportionate number of white and nonpoor students. Conversely, in many of the states with a general public school population that is predominantly white and less poor, charter schools are enrolling a disproportionate percentage of students of color and low-income students. These distinctions also relate to geography, with charter schools in northeastern states serving more poor students and students of color relative to their public schools than do the charter schools in the southwestern states. This may be due to differences in the size and diversity of the public school districts in these different regions. Also, across these different contexts, the more the data are broken down from national- to state- to district- and even neighborhood-level comparisons between charter schools and public schools, the more racially and socioeconomically segregated the charter schools appear to be. For instance, charter schools are often more racially and socioeconomically homogeneous than their local school districts as a whole. And a few studies suggest that charter schools tend to be less diverse than the closest public schools within their districts.

Furthermore, as we explain in the section on access to charter schools, there is some evidence that even in poor communities, the relatively more advantaged of the disadvantaged students are enrolling in charter schools, and the percentage of the lowest-income students served in charter schools across the country is declining. Finally, there is some preliminary evidence to suggest that low-income students and students of color are frequently enrolled in some of the most impoverished charter schools or in those with the least challenging curriculum.

These findings do not necessarily imply that individual charter schools are intentionally segregating students by race and class. Rather, they suggest that the current charter school laws do not foster racial diversity. As we discuss in the section on charter school legislation and diversity, to the extent that the charter school laws vary across states, they almost all allow a great deal of leeway in terms of equity and student access to charter schools. Often the laws' language in these areas is vague and open to different interpretations and, as we mentioned, rarely enforced. In other words, the laws leave room for many charter school founders and educators to do as they wish. Thus, we conclude this chapter with a discussion of implications for policy, noting that if policymakers were to pay attention to public opinion and research that favor less homogeneous schools, charter school laws would need to provide more support and incentives for founders who wanted to create racially/ethnically and socioeconomically diverse charter schools.

Policy Implications and Conclusions

The country is now at an important juncture, uncertain about what, if anything, will replace old race-specific policies, such as school desegregation, and address ongoing racial and social class inequality in our educational system and larger society. In part, charter school laws reflect this ambiguity. Charter schools could play an important role in setting an agenda around these issues, but only if policymakers and charter school movement leaders agree that such issues are worth addressing and amend charter school laws accordingly. If they do not, charter schools across the country will continue to reflect a wide range of local reactions to racial inequality and the national confusion about race and educational policy. Some, perhaps most, of these reactions will exacerbate existing problems.

This will occur because the state laws do not, for the most part, establish the support systems that many of the most disadvantaged students would need—for example, free and accessible transportation or a dissemination system to inform *all* parents about charter school options. Instead, most of the state laws allow charter schools to have some sort of admissions criteria, such as required parent involvement, which often are more difficult for the poorest and most disenfranchised parents to fulfill. And virtually all charter schools have a very limited and narrow method of recruitment that tends to tap into relatively better-off families, even in the low-income communities.

Meanwhile, the legislation generally does not encourage or provide support or incentives for charter school operators to serve a diverse group of students. Therefore, the vast majority of charter schools are created to serve students from a particular cultural or geographic community or those who share a similar educational philosophy or view of parental involvement. Thus, through various subtle recruitment and admissions mechanisms, charter schools are able to attract and admit more homogeneous—along several different dimensions—student bodies.

Layered on top of this are the state and local contexts that have shaped parents' and students' experiences in the regular public schools and their demand for alternatives. We argue that charter schools grow out of a strong sense of frustration with the regular public schools, wherever that frustration may be lodged. In predominantly white and wealthy states with smaller, more separate and unequal school districts—the profile of many of the northern and eastern states—we believe that frustration is housed primarily in the segregated and isolated urban school districts. Thus, we are likely to see charter schools serving poor students and students of color. In more racially and socioeconomically diverse southern and western states that generally contain larger and more diverse school districts, the frustration is likely to transcend a wider range of communities as whites in large urban school districts also want to participate in this reform. Obviously the racial/ethnic and social class inequality in the larger society has framed these frustrations, and if charter school legislation remains as laissez-faire as it has been, this will not be the reform to overcome such inequalities. In fact, it may well be the reform to exacerbate them.

For those charter school supporters who would like to see this reform movement achieve the more progressive goals of greater racial/ethnic and socioeconomic equality for all students, the first step is to reevaluate some of the popular rating systems that are currently applied to charter school laws. For instance, the conservative Center for Education Reform conducts a state ranking of charter school legislation in which the so-called strong laws are the more deregulatory laws that foster the "development of numerous genuinely independent charter schools."[12] The main criteria for these "strong" laws are that they place no (or a very high) limit on the number of charter schools that can open, provide for multiple charter granting agencies, allow students from all over the state to attend, and give schools a great deal of operational autonomy and whether laws allow for an "automatic" waiver from state and district laws and regulations. So-called weak laws, therefore, are those that are more regulatory in terms of all these criteria. The Center ranks all the state charter school laws according to these criteria, thereby designating the "strong" versus the "weak" laws.

Not mentioned in these rankings are any legislative provisions that advance equity or redistribute resources and opportunities to the students who have been the least well served by the public schools. Nor is there any value placed on provisions that would promote what the majority of parents say they want in their public schools—racial and ethnic diversity.

While the Center for Education Reform's ranking system appears to be popular with conservative backers of charter school reform, there are other more liberal and leftist charter school constituents who might be interested in supporting alternative ranking systems. One such system would give states more credit for legislation that requires a certain percentage of charter schools in a state to be racially/ethnically and socioeconomically diverse and then provides financial and resources incentives and supports to allow educators and parents to create such a school. A strong equity-focused law would provide money and resources to allow these diverse charter schools to have broader outreach and recruitment of students from different communities and to provide transportation for each student to and from school. It would restrict the use of parent contracts and disallow the use of admissions criteria, especially criteria based on perceived "ability" and prior achievement. It also would assure that white and wealthy families were not able to use charter school reform to escape racially and socioeconomically diverse public schools and school districts by creating predominantly white charter schools. Meanwhile, it would allow for the creation of some charter schools to enroll mostly African-American, Latino, American-Indian, or other students whose history and culture is often ignored in the regular public schools.

Extra resources and support services would be provided to such schools located in low-income communities to make up for the greater difficulty they face in raising the private resources available in wealthier communities. Still, these laws might want to restrict such extra resources to only those low-income charter schools that are run by community-based educators and parents as opposed to large for-profit educational management organizations (EMOs). Stronger and more specific legislative language giving preference to charter schools serving the most disadvantaged students is also needed.

While we believe that it is not fair to label charter school reform as an elitist movement, we are also aware that it is not realistic to declare charter schools, in their current manifestation, a viable solution to the inequitable educational opportunities available to poor students and students of color within the public schools. We fear that unless charter school laws change to promote more equity, access, and diversity within these more autonomous schools, this reform will become yet another sorting machine that exacerbates the existing system of segregation and isolation along racial/ethnic and social-class lines.

Choosing Segregation

Gordon MacInnes

Polls and interviews do not capture another powerful motivation for the flight of middle-class families to suburbs and to nonpublic schools. (Americans tend to be polite and politically correct in responding to pollsters.) Yes, families leave cities "because the schools are no good," which means for some "because there are too many poor blacks and Latinos in the schools." Many, including many middle-class black families, believe that concentrations of lower-class students disturb the order and dilute the academic standards of schools. For others, the presence of significant numbers of black students of whatever class is sufficient to indicate that the schools are no good and that it is time to move. Dan Goldhaber examined data from the National Educational Longitudinal Study of 1988 to determine the factors most influencing parental choice. He underscores one point: "In all models estimated, the larger the difference between the private and public percent of the student body that is white, the more likely that the private sector is chosen." He concludes that the finding "lends credence to those who argue that school choice could lead to segregation of the school system."[1]

American families increasingly view education as a family asset, something to be bestowed on children like antique silverware or a prized ring. "In the abstract," write David Tyack and Larry Cuban, "people favor giving all children a fair chance, but at the same time they want their children to succeed in the competition for economic and social advantage."[2] That competition means eliminating larger community imperatives for common schooling and diverse classmates if it interferes with the "best" educational option for one's own children. And it

---

Excerpts from Gordon MacInnes, "Kids Who Pick the Wrong Parents and Other Victims of Voucher Schemes," The Century Foundation, New York, 1999.

almost always interferes. As more poor children stay in school for more years, their public schools are punished by the withdrawal of white middle-class students who seek schools with higher test averages and better reputations.

Who Chooses . . . and Who Does Not?

Voucher advocates ignore the lessons of earlier efforts to expand educational opportunity via expanded parental choice. A wide variety of parental choice models have been tried over many years in diverse settings. As the topic of parental choice in general and vouchers in particular has attracted more attention, scholars have sought to identify who actually does the choosing.

The families targeted by voucher advocates as the primary beneficiaries of their proposals—the undereducated very poor—are precisely the families least likely to exercise parental choice. The poorer and the larger the family, the less educated the mother, the less likely that the family will respond to the chance to send their children to better schools.

Parents who participate in choice programs tend to be better educated and to head smaller families than nonparticipating parents, even when incomes are comparable. Not surprisingly then, any kind of parental choice option reduces the proportion of strivers remaining in traditional district schools.

In Montgomery County, Maryland, the school district created nineteen magnet schools with a more rigorous academic program, with the intention of breaking the pattern of residential-neighborhood school segregation by attracting white families. In analyzing the program, Jeffrey Henig found that the specialized academic program may not have had much influence in attracting the relatively few families that opted for magnet schools. Instead, parents seemed drawn to these schools by traditional qualities—safety, an enthusiastic principal and younger faculty, emphasis on good basic instruction—and, coincidentally, academic themes such as foreign languages and culture.[3] White parents tended to pick schools that already had relatively few minority students.[4] Henig found that black parents were motivated more by wanting to keep their kids in predominantly black schools than by wanting them in more challenging academic programs, thus defeating the integrationist goal of the project.[5]

Managing a parental choice program to improve racial diversity is likely to fail, at least if Montgomery County is a reliable guide. St. Louis tells a slightly different story. Since 1983, any black student in the city has been free to transfer to any (predominantly white) school in the surrounding county. In 1996, about 13,500 kids signed up for 120 different schools in St. Louis County, suggesting that a one-way racial diversity strategy can work. Amy Stuart Wells interviewed very small samples of students and parents who elected to stay in all-black city high schools, those who transferred to county schools, and those who returned to city schools after transferring. She reports: "City parents [those whose children remained in St. Louis city schools] . . . absolved themselves of the school choice responsibility, leaving the decision entirely to their adolescent children."[6] Of the students, Wells concludes: "With little parent involvement in their school choices and little emphasis on factors of school quality in discussing their choice, most of the city students have adopted a learn-anywhere achievement ideology."[7] Contrast her findings about the parents of transfer students, whom she found to be "assertive, demanding, and not easily intimidated."[8] As to the students, Wells found that they were "steeped in an achievement ideology that stresses the importance of going to the 'best' school in order to get ahead in life."[9]

The St. Louis return students present a more mixed picture, with some leaving the suburban schools because of disciplinary problems, some because of the inconvenient, early, and long bus trips, and some because they wanted the easier academics and better grades found in all-black city schools. A factor for all the students was the difficulty of fitting into a white culture and the loss of the comfort of familiar settings and friends. The parents of the return students knew very little about the suburban schools and were not extensively involved in their children's decisions to return to the city.[10]

San Antonio has operated three thematic multilingual schools since 1983 in an effort to promote higher achievement among low-income Latino students. Valerie Martinez, Kenneth Godwin, and Frank Kemerer analyzed the socioeconomic backgrounds of parents whose children applied for admission to the magnet schools, and a sample that faithfully reflected San Antonio's demographics of those who did not. They conclude that "the driving forces in becoming a choosing family are the mother's education, high parental educational expectations, and the student's past academic performance."[11] The choosing families were more likely to have some college (32 percent versus 12 percent), less likely to be on welfare (12 percent versus 30 percent), and more likely to have fewer children and higher incomes. As a final bit of evidence of the clear differences between choosing and non-choosing families, the test scores of successful choosers were twice the scores of nonchoosers (113 to 54).[12]

These three experiments with parental choice all point to the same conclusion: Choice is irrelevant—almost definitionally—for children whose parents are incompetent about, or indifferent to, education.

5.

Myth #3: Vouchers Promote Democracy

Vouchers and Citizenship

Richard D. Kahlenberg

The contentious debate over whether public funds should support private schools revolves around a central paradox: Most Americans believe that private schools do a somewhat better job of promoting academic achievement than public schools, but most Americans nevertheless like the *idea* of public education as a means of improving democracy, social cohesion, and national unity.

With the U.S. Supreme Court expected to rule later this year on the constitutionality of a program in Cleveland, Ohio, that uses vouchers to make government funds available to private-school students, and with the Bush administration proposing tuition tax credits in its new budget, advocates of "privatizing" education are now turning their attention to the first principle of how education can and should serve democracy.

Diane Ravitch and Joseph P. Viteritti, professors at New York University who support voucher programs, have produced an edited volume of essays, *Making Good Citizens*, that challenges the conventional view that public education is vital to the nation's civic health. The collection includes an impressive array of authors, not all of whom

Originally published as "Good Schools, Good Citizens," a review of Diane Ravitch and Joseph P. Viteritti, eds., *Making Good Citizens: Education and Civil Society* (New Haven, Conn.: Yale University Press, 2002). Reprinted with permission from *The American Prospect* Volume 13, Number 6: March 25, 2002. *The American Prospect*, 5 Broad Street, Boston, MA 02109.

are explicit advocates of private-school choice, but whose essays, taken as a whole, make an audacious three-part argument that public support for private schools will strengthen democracy in America. The argument's components are that (1) public schools do not produce the populace of critical thinkers that a democracy requires; (2) public education no longer does a good job of assimilating diverse students; and (3) private schools do a better job than public schools of promoting the vibrant civil society that is so important to democracy's success.

Americans widely agree that a good education system is essential to democracy in order to promote intelligent citizens who can govern themselves. As Ravitch puts it: "In a democracy, where government is based on self-rule, every person is a ruler, and all need the education that rulers should have." In addition, according to an essay by Norman Nie and D. Sunshine Hillygus, high educational achievement—particularly high verbal ability on the SAT—promotes an array of desirable behaviors, which are reflected in "political participation, voting turnout, political persuasion, and civil voluntarism." Public schools have failed to raise achievement, Viteritti argues; and in particular, they have perpetuated an achievement gap between races that effectively denies people of color "the full benefits of democratic citizenship."

Several essays in the volume contend that the public schools are failing to teach democratic values and are not helping immigrant students weave their way into the American social fabric. Whereas in the past, Nathan Glazer writes, "the straightforward pursuit of assimilation—'Americanization,' as it was then called—evoked almost no resistance from immigrant parents," today, "the kind of social consensus that allowed the common school to thrive no longer exists." Instead, say Ravitch and Viteritti, public schools encourage "students to identify with their race or their ethnic or cultural origins rather than with the overarching civic ideals of the American community." Likewise, they say, the nation's public schools are not doing a good job of teaching the importance of democracy, instead holding that "everything is relative, simply a matter of taste or preference, and that truth is a social construct [and] that there are no universal standards of right or wrong."

In part the editors blame the failure to promote social cohesion on growing economic and racial segregation in public schools. The old idea of the common school—which would "enroll everyone from all social backgrounds"—was made obsolete when suburbanization produced economically differentiated neighborhoods, says Mark Holmes. Given the persistent racial segregation of public schools, Viteritti writes, "it must seem altogether silly for parents living in racially isolated communities with inferior schools to hear middle-class professionals brood over the threat of social fragmentation" posed by voucher programs. In any event, the old common-school assimilationist model is inequitable, Holmes charges. Opponents of vouchers, he says, "are left defending the dubious ethic of mandatory inculcation of democratic dogma in all children, except those fortunate enough to have affluent parents."

Finally, the collection argues that private schools promote democracy by sustaining Tocqueville's concept of "civil society." Here is the volume's major innovation: Whereas in the past voucher advocates have employed the sterile economic language of "education markets" and "consumers," now vouchers are said to enrich the vital institutions that stand between the state and the market. In this way, the fact that the vast majority of private schools are faith-based turns from a constitutional obstacle to a civic plus. In a pluralistic democracy, public funds should go to support sectarian schools because churches, says Viteritti, "are the backbone of civil society in America." Such, indeed, was the original vision of Americans in the early nineteenth century, before education was "transformed from a civic activity conducted as a private matter to a governmental function overseen by a public bureaucracy."

The remarkable thing about this volume is that one can agree completely with several key premises of the writers—that democracy needs critical thinkers, that we need better ways to encourage identification with America rather than with narrow ethnic groups, that students should be taught the values of democracy and tolerance, and that we need a thriving civil society—and for those very reasons strongly oppose school vouchers.

If we want students who think critically, do we really want parents to use public funds to educate their children at institutions handpicked to replicate the parents' private beliefs (about, say, creationism) rather than to expose students to broader possibilities? If we want to teach children what it means to be an American, do we want public funds to subsidize private schools set up especially to appeal, say, to an Armenian population, or to those seeking an Afrocentric curriculum? What about schools that harden religious differences rather than emphasizing commonality? If we want to teach democracy and equality and tolerance—not just out of a textbook, but in an environment where the lessons are reinforced by the everyday experience of students—do we want to move toward a privatized system that has resulted in greater segregation by race and class when tried in New Zealand, Chile, and the Netherlands? Finally, if we want a rich civil society, with a flourishing religious sector, is it not relevant that our system of strict separation of church and state has long been associated with the strong religious commitment among our citizens?

Surely, American public schools can do more to promote democracy and national identity. To re-create the common school that is economically and racially integrated today requires greater public-school choice to overcome entrenched patterns of residential segregation. But overall the public schools have served us well. The late Albert Shanker, a giant in the field of education and democracy, once wrote:

> A Martian who happened to be visiting Earth soon after the United States was founded would not have given this country much chance of surviving. He would have predicted that this new nation, whose inhabitants were of different races, who spoke different languages, and who followed different religions, wouldn't remain one nation for long. They would end up fighting and killing each other. . . . But that didn't happen. . . . Public schools played a big role in holding our nation together.

Today, we're a more diverse nation than ever—precisely why it's more important than ever to find institutions that bind us together. Significantly, the chasms are bridgeable; indeed, there is strong evidence in William Damon's chapter in this volume that refutes Glazer's claim that we're too diverse for the common school to work anymore. Damon cites a 1999 Public Agenda survey finding that "foreign-born and native-born parents, including whites, African Americans, and Hispanics, share a belief that the United States is a special country. . . . They voice a new patriotism that is calm and inclusive." Strong majorities of all groups, the survey finds, believe in "individual freedom and opportunity, combined with a commitment to tolerance and respect for others," and large numbers say that schools should "teach all children about the ideals and history of the country." Yes, there are inequities in the current system because the wealthy can buy out of our public schools. But while it is one thing for the rich to dig into their own pockets to exercise a constitutional right, it is quite another to ask taxpayers to subsidize a system of vouchers that threatens to undermine the democratic principles and national cohesion we have come to appreciate so much, especially in recent months.

Why School Choice Could Demolish National Unity

Richard Just

Forget the Pledge of Allegiance ruling. The real legal blow of the last few weeks to American patriotism was delivered not by an eccentric panel of Circuit Court judges, but by the U.S. Supreme Court—in its 5-to-4 decision declaring school vouchers constitutional. For years, libertarian conservatives and the religious right have, for different reasons, touted vouchers as the savior of American education. That they still do should come as no shock. But far more surprising is that no segment of the post–September 11 right has risen to question vouchers on the grounds where they are most vulnerable: that they undermine the foundations of American unity—indeed, of American nationalism. You would expect members of an intellectually consistent right wing to be up in arms over any development that threatened our shared sense of national purpose. Unless, of course, mainstream conservatives are deeper in ideological debt to religious nuts and libertarian zealots than to their own principles of patriotism.

It is difficult indeed to find any other explanation for the ridiculous recent parade of conservative commentators bemoaning the Pledge of Allegiance ruling while beating their chests triumphantly over the voucher decision. Have these people forgotten where exactly the Pledge of Allegiance is said? Not in most private or parochial schools, that's for sure. *TAP Online* contacted every private or parochial school in Washington, D.C. Of those where someone spoke to us, only 6 of 26 begin each day by saying the pledge. Five leave the pledge to the

Originally published as "Voucher Nation? Why School Choice Could Demolish National Unity." Reprinted with permission from *The American Prospect* Online: July 11, 2002. *The American Prospect*, 5 Broad Street, Boston, MA 02109.

discretion of individual teachers. And 15—the vast majority—don't say it at all. (And this is the nation's capital. If most private and parochial schools here don't require the pledge, can we expect the statistics to be much better anywhere else?) As I was told when I inquired about the pledge at one Catholic high school, "We say, 'Our Father,' 'Hail Mary,' and that's about it." That may be enough to satisfy the religious right. But do mainstream conservatives who want to replace public schools with private ones really think the Lord's Prayer is an acceptable substitute for the Pledge of Allegiance?

The pledge may be a superficial measure of patriotism, but in this case it points to a serious underlying point: Private schools—especially religious ones—are ill-equipped to play the civic role we expect of education in this country. Without a strong culture of military or civilian service, public schools are the only civic institutions in which most Americans—of all backgrounds—can expect to spend part of their lives. Conservatives are fond of invoking the Declaration of Independence to explain that God has always held an important place in our national discourse. But we might also remember that Thomas Jefferson, author of the Declaration, was a staunch advocate of free, universal public education. He understood that such a system could hold a democratic country together, and he wrote that among the goals of public education was helping each citizen "understand his duties to his neighbors and country, and to discharge with competence the functions confided to him by either." That bit of wisdom is even more relevant today than in Jefferson's time. The United States began life as a fairly homogenous republic, but today we are a democracy of immigrants, a pluralistic society that desperately needs institutions to bind us together. Public schools can and should be the most important of these institutions.

That, at least, is the theory. In practice, we know that American public education is broken—badly. Failing to admit this is where liberals have made both a moral and strategic mistake in the fight against vouchers. I would guess most Americans are intuitively uncomfortable with the idea of disassembling the public-school system and farming out its mission to a host of private schools (that run the gamut from the secular to the religious to the downright kooky). But then they take stock of their neighborhood public school and figure that *anything* would be better than the current situation. Meanwhile, rather than risk cutting themselves off from the campaign donations of teachers' unions by acknowledging that the tenure system and other anti-meritocratic protections are the biggest impediments to improving our schools, liberals have allowed themselves to become defenders of a mediocre status quo in American education. Given a choice between voucher-worshipping conservatives who want to destroy the public schools and liberals who appear to think nothing is wrong, it is unsurprising that many Americans—including Democrats—want to give vouchers a chance.

It is now up to liberals to explain why this would be a disaster and to provide alternatives that seek to preserve public education rather than destroy it. (Declaring a public war on teacher protections that privilege seniority over competency would be a bold first step.) In failing systems—the kind that vouchers are supposed to help—the primary alternatives to public schools are often religious ones. So the inane logic of vouchers would leave us with a stark choice: Either become a country that pays religious institutions to proselytize to children of other faiths, or become a country that educates children of different religions separately. One option undermines the spirit of the U.S. Constitution. The other undermines the spirit of American patriotism. Conservatives have long clung to the notion of an American melting pot. But what kind of melting pot will our society be if Protestants, Catholics, Jews, and Muslims are educated separately in their own schools? If ever there was a sinister way to weaken American patriotism borne of pluralism, this is it.

As for conservatives, no one expects theocrats such as Pat Robertson or Gary Bauer to defend principles of American unity over the interests of religious extremists. And no one expects the Cato Institute to defend patriotism over the religion of free markets. But there must be some reasonable conservatives—and here I am looking in the direction of national greatness conservatives and McCain followers, neither fundamentalists nor libertarians—who recognize the hypocrisy of rallying around the Pledge of Allegiance while undermining the ability of public schools to serve as temples of American values and ideals. Or have years of unholy alliance with religious extremists permanently blinded them to the fact that America's future depends not just on our ability to be *under God* but to be *one nation, indivisible* as well?

Religious Schooling with Public Dollars

Gordon MacInnes

Religious schools are founded primarily to inculcate particular religious or sectarian values, not to provide an academically rigorous program to all comers. Although some religious schools are only loosely associated with their founders, it is likely that the religious schools most accessible to the poor students who would need to use vouchers are among those that retain a strong commitment to religious education. Most religious schools are religious by purpose, curriculum, and in the commitment of their leadership.

For most of the last fifty years or so there has been a steady and still unresolved constitutional debate about the relationship of religious schools and the expenditure of tax dollars. [This issue was finally resolved in 2002 when the U.S. Supreme Court permitted a voucher program that aids religious private schools in Cleveland. See *Zelman v. Simmons-Harris.]* The thread of Supreme Court decisions is not straight or consistent, but the prevailing Court doctrine sets forth three tests that were handed down in the 1971 decision *Lemon v. Krutzman.* To pass muster, a public program that spends tax dollars in a religious school must (1) be found to have "a secular legislative purpose," (2) have a "principal or primary effect" that neither advances nor inhibits religion, and (3) not result in "excessive government entanglement with religion." Voucher proponents seem quite relaxed about the issue, appearing confident that the nation's struggle with these vexing issues is to be easily resolved (Chubb and Moe devote a single paragraph to the matter in their 229-page book).

Excerpts from Gordon MacInnes, "Kids Who Pick the Wrong Parents and Other Victims of Voucher Schemes," The Century Foundation, New York, 1999.

Simply put, if religious schools are excluded from vouchers, then there is no choice. In the 1993–94 school year, fully half (50.6 percent) of all students attending nonpublic schools were enrolled in Catholic schools; an additional 34 percent attended other religious schools (Episcopal, Lutheran, and Evangelical Christian being the largest). The remaining nonpublic students are found in nonsectarian, independent schools, most of which have no interest in voucher students.[1] In fact, the leaders of many secular, independent schools oppose vouchers.

The existence of large numbers of Catholic schools in city neighborhoods is cited as proof that voucher parents will have ample choices. In fact, Catholic schools are affected by two powerful demographic trends. The first is the decline since the early 1960s in the number of schools and students. In 1960, there were 12,893 Catholic schools enrolling 5.25 million students; by 1997, the number of schools had declined by 36 percent (to 8,223) and students by 52.4 percent (to 2.6 million). The second is that Catholic schools attract students who are more likely to be non-Catholics and from a higher socioeconomic status than was true in the 1950s and 1960s. This is not terribly surprising in that many schools in inner-city neighborhoods closed as white Catholics moved to the suburbs; in the Catholic schools that remain, there has been an influx of Protestant African Americans seeking alternatives to the public schools. Since 1972, there has been a lockstep increase in non-Catholic and nonwhite enrollments, the former increasing from about 2 percent to 13.6 percent, the latter from 5 percent to 12.3 percent.[2] However, this trend has leveled off in the last decade as black student enrollment has declined from 8.6 percent (234,300) in 1987 to 8.1 percent (213,670) in 1997.[3]

Suburban Catholic schools serve a demand for religious orientation, stronger academic emphasis than can be found in public high schools, and, frequently, strong athletic teams. Typically, families seeking such schools tend to be from the upper-income and educational cohorts (almost half—45 percent—come from the top quartile of the income distribution, and about one-fifth from households with incomes above $75,000, versus 7 percent of public school students).[4] Suburban Catholic schools are much more likely to have waiting lists and thus to be a weak alternative for poor city voucher students.

What is yet to be tested is the tolerance of American voters for voucher policies that favor the interests of religious schools over the needs of poor, minority city kids who are supposedly the intended beneficiaries. As we learned in the discussion of existing capacity, most religious schools report that they will not participate in public programs that require them to accept public school students randomly, or if the students present special needs, or are given the right to exempt themselves from religious instruction and observances. Will voters approve programs where there is no clear, secular legislative purpose being served? How does a state enforce public purposes without entangling itself in the operations of religious schools? Voucher advocates have avoided the nettlesome situations that are bound to arise if religious schools are broadly and smoothly included in voucher programs.

The experiences of Cleveland and Milwaukee force attention to this question by weight of the number of religious schools participating and the fact that the low voucher payments force parents into low-tuition religious schools (80 percent of Cleveland voucher students attend religious schools). Public schools teach a rough equality and single-heritage credo by accepting all comers and mixing everyone, even if only between classes or in the cafeteria line. Religious schools exist to teach that we should be aware of differences and of the superiority of one faith over all others. Thus is America's civic culture—always fragile—further endangered.

The early experience in Cleveland offers little comfort to voucher advocates. The three "problem" schools are all religious. The Golden Christian Academy relies entirely on Christian educational videotapes for its classroom instruction, which is overseen by parent volunteers.[5] Two Islamic academies were found to be operating in unsafe facilities (one with a convicted murderer on staff) and with unlicensed teachers.[6] Consider these possible examples:

- Orthodox Jewish, evangelical Protestant, and other religiously zealous schools that actively exclude all but their believers from admission

- Islamic schools organized by the Fruit of Islam that teach an anti-white, separatist curriculum

- Evangelical schools that teach a creationist science curriculum that excludes evidence of evolution and genetics

- Sects like the Church of Scientology that teach a cult of personality in the name of religion

- Any religious instruction that sets its believers apart from the American mainstream and condemns nonbelievers

True, Americans display great tolerance and reverence for the First Amendment, but that is not the same as subsidizing instruction in divisive, absolutist, or un-American dogma with tax funds.

In most cities and for most voucher holders, Catholic schools are likely to be the most accessible option. While research is at best muddled regarding the *educational* advantages of a Catholic education, there is reason to believe that most of the advantages for urban students are found at the high school level. The voucher movement assumes that parents are in the best position to determine their children's educations and that they will select "better" schools. Presumably, the same phenomena must govern the present market for nonpublic schooling; that is, Catholic schools with good reputations are the ones that already attract the most students, and those of lesser quality are the ones with the most openings. In fact, 40 percent of Catholic schools presently have waiting lists for admission, and one must assume that they are the better schools by reputation and in the quality of education they offer (they also tend to be in the suburbs).[7] *One unintended consequence of voucher programs, then, would be to sustain low-quality Catholic schools that otherwise would be closed for insufficient demand.*

One is struck by how superficial the public debate has been on the complexity and difficulty of large subsidies for those attending religious schools. If vouchers are truly intended to assist those who are the least served by public schools, then it is not likely that religious schools can be the main exit option for city parents. Unless religious schools are prepared to go back on their religious origins in exchange for public funds or the public endorses subsidies for religious indoctrination, the seats envisaged by voucher advocates simply won't be there.

6.

Myth #4: American Public Is Clamoring for Vouchers

Vouchers and Public Opinion

Ruy Teixeira

On June 27, 2002, the Supreme Court ruled that the Cleveland school voucher program, which allowed vouchers to be used to attend religious schools, was constitutional. Since one of the big problems always faced by voucher supporters was the possible unconstitutionality of allowing publicly funded vouchers to be used to attend such schools, they were understandably delighted. President Bush also weighed in on the ruling, comparing its import to the 1954 *Brown v. Board of Education* decision that ended separate but equal schooling. He indicated his desire to make a strong public push for vouchers, a departure from his reserved rhetoric about the issue during the 2000 campaign and his quick jettisoning of a voucher component in his education reform bill.

Is he (or maybe Karl Rove) onto something? Will the Court decision open the floodgates for a voucher movement that will sweep the nation? Possible but not very likely. The simple fact is that vouchers are not particularly popular, and the reasons for that lack of popularity have never had much to do with worries about their constitutional status. Therefore, the Court's decision is unlikely to change the political outlook for vouchers.

General Views of Public Education

The lack of popularity of vouchers has several root causes. First, consider the fact that the public is actually pretty happy with the public schools its children attend. In the latest Phi Delta Kappa (PDK)/Gallup poll, an annual benchmark survey on public opinion and education, 71 percent gave the public school their eldest child attends an A or a B. That does not suggest the kind of widespread parental disgust with schools that might fuel a voucher movement.

On the other hand, it is true that the public judges the nation's schools as a whole much more harshly. In the same poll, only 24 percent of the public gave the nation's schools an A or B, and 63 percent assigned a grade of C or lower.

Why this dramatic difference? How can people rate the nation's public schools so poorly and their own children's schools so highly? My interpretation of these data is that, even allowing for considerable bias, people just do not have the sense of crisis about their local public schools—reflecting fairly positive personal experiences with them—that they have about the national system. On the other hand, they may have read about truly dysfunctional schools elsewhere—inner-city public schools would be the most common example—and may well consider this a very serious problem. So when they criticize the nation's public schools, they may be expressing a sincere judgment about schools' failure to lift up a substantial proportion of society from disadvantaged circumstances, not just transferring their own personal dissatisfaction onto a national target. That would contradict a common picture of the typical citizen as narrowly self-interested and unconcerned with the collective welfare, but there is plenty of precedent for this view in the scholarly literature.

Some support for this interpretation is provided by data from a 2001 Educational Testing Service (ETS) poll. In separate questions, respondents were asked how good schools were in high-, middle-, and low-income areas. Sixty-nine percent of the public rated schools in high-income areas "excellent" or "good," 80 percent of the public thought schools in middle-income areas were "good" or "fair," and 56 percent thought schools in low-income areas were "inadequate" or "in crisis" (another 26 percent rated them fair, and just 12 percent thought there were good or excellent). Thus, the public's views of schools in these different areas tracks pretty closely with what we know about school performance. This finding strongly suggests that the popular attitude toward the nation's schools overall is driven by perceptions of failing performance in low-income areas. Conversely, the public's positive assessment of schools in their own areas probably reflects the fact the most parents live in middle- or high-income areas, where the schools are actually pretty good.

SUPPORT FOR PUBLIC SCHOOLS. Consistent with these relatively positive personal experiences, support for the institution of public schools remains strong. In the 2002 Gallup/PDK poll, 69 percent said we should concentrate on reforming the existing public school system; just 27 percent said we should focus on finding an alternative system. Similarly, and very much to the point of the vouchers issue, 69 percent of the public said they would prefer a plan that improved and strengthened the existing public schools, compared to only 29 percent who believed a plan for providing vouchers would be better.

Other data reinforce these findings. In a June 1999 Penn, Schoen and Berland/Democratic Leadership Council (PSB/DLC) poll, 71 percent endorsed using all available resources to improve public schools, compared to just 24 percent who preferred helping people go to private schools. Even more impressive, a staggering 98 percent say they favor continuing the guarantee of a free public education, and 96 percent say it is important that public schools be strengthened (1998 Peter Harris/Recruiting New Teachers [RNT] poll).

Thus, general support for reforming and strengthening the public schools seems strong. But just what kind of reform does the public have in mind? This is a vast subject, but in some respects it can be boiled down to two words: standards and resources.

STANDARDS AND RESOURCES. Possibly the clearest public preference about school reform is the desire for higher standards and the willingness to tolerate fairly strict guidelines and testing regimes to accomplish this goal. In a 2002 ETS survey, 73 percent of adults favor testing student achievement and holding teachers and school administrators responsible for what children learn. And in the 2002 PDK/Gallup poll, two-thirds of the public backed a key provision from the No Child Left Behind Act, an education reform that mandated the tracking of student progress from grades three to eight by means of an annual standardized test.

There is some evidence that support for standards today is substantially higher than it has been in the past. For example, a question dating back to the late 1950s asks people whether students should have to pass a standard, nationwide academic examination to graduate from high school. The public was split on the question through the mid-1960s, but by the mid-1970s (the next time the question was asked) a strong consensus had evolved: by more than a 2:1 ratio, people favored having such an examination. That support continues to the present day and, if anything, is becoming more lopsided.

So support for educational standards is rock-solid. But, as shown by the same 2002 ETS survey, the public believes that, while we need accountability, we cannot reform education without more resources for the public school system. Eighty-five percent of the public supports hiring more teachers to reduce class size (75 percent say they would favor this even if it meant increased taxes), 80 percent support raising salaries to hire and retain good teachers, and 71 percent support using more taxpayer funds to build and repair schools.

A 2002 Ipsos-Reid poll for the Committee for Education Funding further documents the strong support for investment in our educational system. When respondents were asked what should be the number-one federal spending priority this year, aside from spending on the military and homeland security, more chose education (38 percent) than any other area, including prescription drug benefits (25 percent) and tax cuts (just 14 percent). In an interesting exercise, the survey told respondents that we spend about 2.5 cents per dollar of the federal budget on education and asked their opinion of spending 5 cents per dollar (in other words, doubling the amount). The response was overwhelmingly positive: 54 percent supported the notion, 30 percent thought we should actually spend *more*, and just 15 percent thought 5 cents per dollar would be too much. Even making allowances for the somewhat abstract nature of the exercise (there is no mention of budget allocations in total dollar terms), the level of positive response for such a radical spending increase is still impressive. It also is worth noting that a February Ipsos-Reid poll for the same group found 69 percent of the public supporting deficit spending if it was necessary to fund educational improvement adequately.

Finally, the survey asked respondents to rate different reasons to increase spending on education. Topping the list was improving recruitment and retention of quality teachers, consistent with other poll findings over the past several years. Intriguingly, the second most popular reason was "to give students from low income families equal access to the opportunities education provides" (with 60 percent saying "a very good reason" and another 28 percent saying "a fairly good reason"). This result suggests that the public's support for increased education spending is motivated by concerns that go beyond their own children and community.

In still another sign of support for increased spending on education, the 2002 Gallup/PDK poll found lack of funding topping the list of problems that public schools in respondents' communities had to deal with. That reverses a trend of many years in which troubles like lack of discipline and drug use tended to top the list.

The findings from these polls are especially significant since they were taken *after* passage of the No Child Left Behind Act, which focused tightly on raising standards. Many in Congress now argue that the heavy emphasis on standards in the recently passed education reform law needs to be supplemented by a generous infusion of resources into the educational system. These data show that the public is sympathetic to such a viewpoint.

VOUCHERS

So most of the public likes its local schools, and, while people support stiffer standards, they believe that meeting those standards and the general goal of a good education will require an augmenting of resources for the school system. Small wonder, then, that vouchers, generally believed to be a drain on funding for the public schools, do not generate a lot of public enthusiasm.

Consider the following. The Gallup/Phi Delta Kappa annual poll on education, probably the best source of public opinion data on education issues, shows support for vouchers increasing from 1993/94 to 1998, dropping from 1998 to 2001, and then rising in 2002 (note that this was prior to the Supreme Court decision) but at no time demonstrating any strongly pro-voucher sentiment. Gallup/PDK has been asking this question for a number of years: "Do you favor or oppose allowing students and parents to choose a private school to attend at public expense?" Even in 2002, after the uptick between 2001 and 2002, the response was 52 percent opposed and 46 percent in favor. The average response from the 1998 peak to today has been 55 percent opposed and 41 percent in favor.

An alternative wording by Gallup/PDK elicited a somewhat more positive response on vouchers, but the pattern remains the same: rising support until 1998, falling support from 1998 to 2001, increasing support again in 2002, but no evidence of strong pro-voucher sentiment. This question talked about allowing parents to send children to any "public, private or church-related school," with government picking up all or part of the tuition for nonpublic school choices. In this case, the response in 2002 was 52 percent favorable and 46 percent opposed, and the 1998–2002 average was exactly split: 49 percent in favor and 49 percent opposed.

Such inconclusive results are common in public opinion research on vouchers. By and large, questions that emphasize taxpayer or public expense and full funding of private school tuition tend to elicit slightly negative responses (the first Gallup/PDK question), while those that deemphasize the source of voucher money or allude to partial, rather than full, coverage of tuition (the second question) generate more positive responses. But the close division of the public in either case suggests a policy that is not particularly popular, no matter how it is presented to the public.

And the types of questions that evoke negative responses are consistent with the idea that vouchers' chief political vulnerability is voters' fear that they would drain money and resources from the public schools. Indeed, follow-up questions that have been done in some surveys show just how soft expressed support for vouchers is when confronted with the possibility the public schools might lose funding as a result. In a June/July 1999 Kaiser/NPR/Kennedy School of Government survey, respondents were asked: "Do you favor or oppose the government offering parents money or 'vouchers' to send their children to private or religious schools, or public schools outside their district, or haven't you heard enough about that to have an opinion?" This produced a typically split response—31 percent in favor and 36 percent opposed—but note that 33 percent said they had not heard enough to have an opinion. The 31 percent in favor can reasonably be said to be the most well-informed and presumably committed voucher supporters. These pro-voucher respondents were then asked the follow-up question: "Would you still favor this if it meant there would be less money for public schools in your area?" In this context, only about half (52 percent) said they would still support vouchers, while 44 percent moved into opposition.

This is exactly why voucher programs fare so poorly in referenda, where the issue of loss of funding for public schools is typically key to the arguments of voucher opponents. In fact, in 2000 vouchers lost in California by 71 to 29 percent and in Michigan by 69 to 31 percent in referendum campaigns where the drain on public funding for schools was the critical issue. There is no reason to believe that voucher referenda will fare any better today since the public is, if anything, more supportive of school funding than it was several years ago.

But what if vouchers were means-tested—that is, tilted toward low-income families, who are presumably most in need of escape from bad public schools? Would the public be any more supportive of such a system? Not on the evidence of current polling data. In 2002 both ABC News and the Associated Press asked questions along these lines, and both polls found that making vouchers available just to low-income families met with a tepid response that then changed to outright opposition if it was posited that the public schools would lose some funding as a result. The ABC News poll showed close to an even split on the basic proposition (50 percent in favor and 47 percent opposed), but 42 percent of those in favor expressed opposition if such vouchers meant losses in public school funding. That brought total opposition to the proposal to 68 percent, with just 29 percent in favor.

Of course, none of this gainsays the fair amount of support out there for some of the ideas behind vouchers—chiefly, that of choice in general and the ability of parents to opt out of poorly performing schools in particular. The latter helps explain why blacks, and especially poor blacks, tend to be unusually driven to back vouchers. Would the public be more supportive of a system that provided more choice but did not appear to pose the danger of draining funds from public schools? There is good evidence to suppose they would. For example, in a 1999 Penn Schoen Berland/Democratic Leadership Council poll, the public preferred allowing parents with children in low-performing schools to send those children to the public school they think best rather than allowing them to make use of alternative schools, including private schools (58 to 33 percent).

That brings up the topic of public school choice. While there has been relatively little polling on this subject, it is striking how uniformly positive public reaction tends to be. A variety of question wordings have been used since 1987, and they all return strong evidence of public support—from a low of 60 percent to a high of 82 percent in favor of public school choice. There also is some indication of increasing favor from 1989 onward. In terms of demographics, results that are available from a 1997 survey suggest that backing for this approach is stronger at lower education and income levels, not surprising given that the most affluent areas tend to have the best neighborhood schools. But even among the affluent support is still solid—just not as much so as among the less privileged.

Even so ardent a proponent of vouchers as Terry Moe, the Stanford professor who coauthored (with John Chubb) the seminal book on the topic, *Politics, Markets, and America's Schools*, has to admit that evidence from his own survey (presented in his 2001 book *Schools, Vouchers, and the American Public*) shows the public much more sympathetic to public school choice than to vouchers. In his survey, 69 percent of the public prefers public school choice within school districts and 75 percent favors choice outside of districts if space is available, compared to 60 percent support for vouchers (and that stemming from a question crafted to produce a sympathetic response). Significantly, the very parents who typically are held up the chief beneficiaries of vouchers, inner-city parents, are almost unanimous (84 to 88 percent) in their support for public school choice.

Conclusion: Reform, Not Vouchers

The public remains supportive of the public school system despite its having criticisms of that system's current performance, particularly with regard to how the system serves poor students. It does want to see that performance improved, starting with higher standards, and is willing to tolerate fairly strict guidelines and testing regimes, such as those in the 2002 No Child Left Behind Act, to accomplish this goal. But the public recognizes that tougher standards and the general quest for educational excellence mean more money has to be spent on public schools—for example, to reduce class size, to attract better teachers, and to modernize school infrastructure.

The data presented here suggest that the public is far more interested in seeing this dual agenda of standards and resources implemented than in moving to a voucher-based system. Indeed, vouchers tend to lose badly today as political propositions precisely because they are perceived as being in conflict with the second part of that agenda. Therefore, only failure of the political system to follow through with policies to meet people's aspirations for the public schools is likely to generate serious popular backing for vouchers in the long run.

In the meantime, the widespread interest in selecting schools and, in particular, the ability of parents to opt out of poorly performing ones, apparently can be served by moving to expand public school choice. The data suggest the nation, and particularly those parents with children in poorly performing schools, would welcome such an expansion.

Congress and School Vouchers

Thad Hall

Just as it is possible to size up public support for any given policy idea by looking to opinion polls, one can gauge a proposal's political viability by examining the behavior of Congress. Everyone recognizes that members of Congress are most interested in one thing: keeping their jobs. One way that they do this is by supporting popular policy positions, so members often decide which side of an issue to be on by measuring the pulse of their constituents.

This chapter examines how Congress has treated school vouchers—or what conservatives prefer to call "school choice"—over the past decade. What is clear from examining the issue is that members of Congress typically have taken great pains to avoid debating school vouchers, and when they have, vouchers have gone down to defeat. Opposition to vouchers is not just found in the Democratic Party; it extends to Republicans as well, especially Republican moderates. It is an issue that the GOP leadership in the House and Senate generally has kept off of the agenda, unlike other instances where Republicans have forced Democrats to go on the record and vote against what they deemed a popular measure. In short, although conservatives in Congress may support vouchers rhetorically, they have not put their money where their mouths are when it comes to the legislative process.

Vouchers as Symbols

The first way that members of Congress try to make political points is through bill introductions. When someone in Congress wants to get an issue on the legislative agenda, he or she does this by introducing a bill and getting fellow legislators to cosponsor it. In every Congress more than ten thousand bills are introduced, with fewer than four hundred typically becoming law in recent years; most of the rest serve a symbolic purpose, showing that the member has taken a stand on the issue. For example, for more than twenty years Congressman James Oberstar (D.-MN) has been introducing legislation to ban abortions. This bill is never acted on, but introducing it provides Oberstar with an opportunity to make a statement.

Support for educational vouchers has become something of a litmus test for conservatives in recent years. The Heritage Foundation, the Cato Institute, and other conservative/libertarian think tanks have made vouchers a focus of their education reform agenda. For them, the answer to the question "How to improve public education?" is simple—privatize it by giving out vouchers to let students attend private schools. This argument by conservative policy institutes has become part of the broader right-wing political agenda in recent years, as books and opinion pieces have touted the seemingly costless benefits of school vouchers as a means of improving education.

Of course, an idea is only an idea unless it is acted on and implemented as public policy. The debate over the efficacy of school vouchers is an academic exercise until it is applied and schoolchildren actually are allowed to use vouchers to attend the school of their choice. While small-scale voucher experiments are currently being conducted—for instance, in Milwaukee and Cleveland—the most efficient way of implementing public policy in the United States is to do it at the federal level, where it can make an impact on the lives of people on a continental scale.

With this in mind, the goal for conservatives should be to use federal education policy as a vehicle for taking vouchers nationwide. One way to measure the support that vouchers have in Congress is to examine the number of education bills promoting public school vouchers that have been introduced into Congress over the past decade and the number of sponsors these bills attract. The data show that the number of school voucher bill introductions and cosponsors did increase as the number of Republicans in the House increased. This is not surprising; the freshman class of the 104th Congress was more conservative and more ideological than other Republicans in Congress, with many of them having been influenced by GOPAC, the conservative action group headed by Republican leader Newt Gingrich (R.-GA). However, as the Republican Party has come to control Congress over the past eight years, something interesting has happened: the number of voucher bills has declined from a high of nineteen in the 106th Congress to eleven in the 107th.

Considering that less than 20 percent of all legislation passes a vote in either chamber and less than 5 percent of all bills become law, the aggregate numbers of bill introductions, while interesting, do not tell the entire story. The bigger question is this: Could conservatives take their control of Congress and the legislative agenda and use it to press the case for implementing school vouchers nationally?

Voucher Debates in Congress

School vouchers have been debated in Congress a number of times since the early 1990s, when President George H. W. Bush made a limited school voucher program a part of his education reform proposal. Opposition to vouchers came from the usual corners, such as from Senator Edward Kennedy (D.-MA), but also from Republicans in Congress. Senator Nancy Kassebaum (R.-KS) was concerned that in practice a school choice plan that included private schools would result in transportation costs that "could grow and grow," making the implementation of choice unfeasible. Similarly, Representative Bill Goodling (R.-PA), the ranking minority member of the Education and Labor Committee, stated, "If you have 500 students in a school and 250 of them are the 'thousand points of light' and decide to go to a school of choice, that leaves 250 fallen angels behind."[1]

There was a vote on a very limited school choice plan sponsored by Senator Orrin Hatch (R.-UT) that would have allowed for a $30 million private-public school choice demonstration program, but the Senate rejected the proposal by a 57–36 vote. Six Republicans voted against the Hatch amendment, including several from the northeast.[2]

Vouchers fared no better in 1993 when they came up during the debate over the Goals 2000: Educate America Act. When Representative Dick Armey (R.-TX) offered an amendment in the House Education and Labor Committee to spend $393 million to fund public, private, and parochial school choice programs, it was defeated 35–7; he could not even garner the support of half of the Republican members of the committee.[3]

The defeat of the Armey amendment occurred before the 1994 election returns, which brought Republicans majorities in the House and Senate. With public opinion polls consistently ranking education as one of the top issues in America—and with vouchers being a pressing issue for the conservative movement—one would have expected vouchers to be a priority when Republicans gained control of Congress and its policy agenda in 1995 and could thus bring up bills in committee and on the floor whenever they wanted. However, school vouchers have been conspicuously absent from the congressional landscape since the "Republican revolution." There has been a paucity of votes on the issue over the past eight years.

One might argue that this was the case during the Clinton administration because Republicans knew that the president would veto any school voucher bill. However, this argument falls flat taking into consideration how Republicans pressed for passage of legislation banning so-called "partial birth abortions" throughout the late 1990s. Republicans used the controversy as a "key vote," designed to force Democrats to go on the record about their position on this type of abortion procedure. Republicans held similar votes on tax cuts in order to use them against Democratic candidates in elections. If vouchers were the potent political issue that conservative think tanks want to believe, one would expect there to be repeated "key votes" on the matter.

In fact, Republicans were not bringing voucher bills to the floor every year, trying to make Democrats defend their opposition to them. GOP congressional leadership could not even get members of its own party to support voucher plans. The debate that occurred in the House on November 4, 1997, is an example of the policy meltdown that voucher advocates in Congress have had to contend with. On that date, Republicans in the House proposed the Helping Empower Low-Income Parents (HELP) scholarship program, which would have let families with incomes below 185 percent of the federal poverty rate use money from Washington—a $310 million fund would have been established—to send their children to private and parochial schools. Even with both Speaker Gingrich and Majority Leader Armey making strong speeches in support of the bill, it was soundly defeated, 228–191. Thirty-five Republicans voted against the voucher proposal, many of them unsurprisingly moderates such as Nancy Johnson (R.-CT), Michael Castle (R.-DE), and Jim Leach (R.-IA). During the debate, Marge Roukema (R.-NJ) expressed concern that "ultimately, these vouchers will result in gutting the public school system."

The only successful floor vote on school vouchers occurred in 1998, when the House voted to include funding for a voucher program that would allow any student in the District of Columbia to attend any public or private school. However, this "success" was not very promising for voucher advocates for two reasons. First, the House position was not included in the final bill; the D.C. appropriations bill that the president signed included no language about school vouchers. Second, although the bill passed, it did not secure a majority of all members of the House. A total of 214 members supported the measure, and 208 opposed it (13 members did not vote). This lack of support is even more stark taking into account that the bill affected no voting member of the House, as the District is not represented by a vote in Congress. Once more the speaker and the majority leader pressed hard to build support for this bill but were not able to secure a strong majority, in large measure because fifteen Republicans again voted for public schools and against vouchers.

With President Clinton in office, congressional Republicans knew that they would not be able to get a voucher proposal enacted into law. However, with the election of President George W. Bush, it would seem that voucher supporters finally had the political environment that they desired—a Republican Congress and a Republican president. The timing was made even better by the fact that the Elementary and Secondary Education Act (ESEA), which is the primary vehicle for funding public education in the United States, was up for reauthorization in 2001. President Bush had campaigned in favor of school vouchers, and his proposal for reauthorizing ESEA included a voucher provision. The proposal attracted immediate support in Congress from pro-voucher advocates, such as House majority whip Tom DeLay, who said, "America now has a president who understands the problems afflicting our nation's education system."[4]

However, even during the Bush transition it was obvious that the president would give up on his voucher proposal. Even as Ari Fleischer, the president's spokesperson, stressed that "school choice is, indeed, a component of what President-elect Bush believes needs to be done to improve our schools. He stands by it," the president was planning to drop it. Why? As Senator Judd Gregg (R.-NH) noted, any school voucher proposal "would be a tough one to pass." With at least thirty-five House Republicans likely to vote against the president and the Democrats united in opposition, the votes simply were not there. Darcy Olsen of the Cato Institute remarked, "[Vouchers are] not something people are going to go to the mat on." So even in the optimal political environment—unified Republican control of government, vouchers still are an untenable policy position.[5]

During the debate on the president's No Child Left Behind education reform bill, Senator Gregg offered a pilot school choice plan for disadvantaged students. The amendment was defeated 58–41, with a diverse group of Democrats and Republicans refusing to back it. Traditional, moderate Republican opponents of vouchers, including Senators Susan Collins and Olympia Snowe of Maine, voted against the amendment, but so did conservative Republicans from rural states like Mike Enzi of Wyoming and Conrad Burns of Montana. The defeat of the Gregg amendment, which in many ways parroted the language the president had employed when he first sent his bill to Capitol Hill, signaled how little support vouchers have in Congress today.

As of this writing, Republicans are pushing legislation to supplement vouchers in the District of Columbia, but notably they are limiting this effort to a constituency that has no real voice in Congress.

Tax Subsidies for Private School Students

Although school vouchers have proved to be a political nonstarter in Congress, there has been some support for other means of giving individuals assistance in sending their children to private school. The most popular of these efforts has been education savings accounts (ESA), which also have been referred to as educational IRAs. An ESA is a simple concept. Money is contributed to a special account up to a ceiling of $2,000 and, as long as it is used for the education of a child or grandchild, the principal and interest can be withdrawn tax-free. However, unlike a traditional IRA, the contribution itself cannot be deducted against income. Of course, a tax break on the interest earned on $2,000 is paltry, as anyone with a traditional savings account knows.

Conservatives have been touting ESAs since the mid-1990s. They were first successful in 1997, when the House passed legislation that would allow parent, grandparents, and scholarship sponsors to contribute up to $2,500 annually to ESAs. The House vote was 230 to 198,[6] with 15 Democrats joining 215 Republicans in supporting the bill. The legislation languished in the Senate because conservatives, led by Senator Paul Coverdell (R.-GA), were unable to overcome the threat of a filibuster by Democrats.[7]

The argument against this legislation was different from the line of attack used against school vouchers. Opponents argued that ESAs subsidize private education for the rich. As Representative Martin Frost (D.-TX) asserted, "This [bill] only helps one class of people—upper income constituents who live in the suburbs and send their children to private schools."

However, this reasoning against ESAs was not as persuasive as the points made about school vouchers taking funds away from public schools and giving them to private ones. By 1998, both the House and Senate passed bills allowing families to place $2,000 annually in ESAs, from which it could be withdrawn for a variety of purposes, including private school tuition, tutoring, home computers, and transportation expenses. Again the bill passed the House with 12 Democrats joining 213 Republicans.[8] In the Senate, 8 Democrats joined 51 Republicans voting in favor.[9] Only a veto by President Clinton kept the ESA bill from becoming law.[10]

With the election of George W. Bush, the enactment of ESA legislation was ensured. ESAs were included in the Economic Growth and Tax Relief Reconciliation Act of 2001. Under the law, parents, grandparents, scholarship sponsors, and corporations are allowed to contribute annually into an ESA. These funds can be used for public or private educational purposes. However, the main beneficiaries are children in private schools; 52 percent of the benefits go to the 7 percent of families with children in private school. However, the Republican victory here is somewhat hollow, as the typical tax savings on these accounts ranges between $7 and $37 annually.[11]

Conclusions

The debate in Congress is illustrative of the problems that vouchers have more broadly: as a policy solution, they just are not popular. Time and again over the past decade, voucher proposals have gone down to swift and sharp defeat. Voucher opponents are distributed across the political spectrum; they are not just liberal Democrats. Even some conservative Republicans in the Rocky Mountain region have signaled their objections. Their constituents have little to gain from such proposals because the logistical challenges of implementing a meaningful voucher program in a rural area are daunting.

Members of Congress work very hard to get elected and reelected, and staying on the right side of the issues with voters is critical to electoral success. The failure of vouchers in Congress reflects the fact that most Americans do not support them, and there is no popular pressure for Congress to take federal money out of public schools and put it into voucher schemes. As the debate over the No Child Left Behind bill showed, even with a Republican Congress, a Republican president, and conservative activists all beating the drum in support of vouchers, only 41 percent of the Senate could be mustered to support so much as a trial program on a national level.

Part II. The Public School Choice Alternative

This section of the book proposes a set of public school choice policies that seek to avoid the pitfalls of vouchers while garnering the benefits. The authors contend that public school choice, if properly structured, will allow poor children to escape bad schools, will provide more variety in schooling, and can shake up the bureaucracy with competitive pressures. At the same time, such policies can raise student achievement, facilitate racial and economic integration, foster social cohesion, and promote democratic values. For all these reasons, public school choice is more popular with the American public than private school vouchers.

7.

Overview

Progressive Alternatives to School Vouchers

Brent Staples, Christopher Edley, Jr.,
Elliot Mincberg, and Adam Urbanski

Brent Staples: I live in New York City and I've lived there for 15 years—and, not that you need to know this, but I'm about to be married, and I've inherited a teenage stepson, who is, in fact, black, and I've sat down with my wife-to-be and I said, "What are we going to do with this kid? He needs some work. He's been in a bad school in this area, which will be unnamed. He's going to come to New York." And what were our options for a black kid in New York who needs some special attention. And, of the two schools that I had to choose from that he could test into—Stuyvesant and Bronx Science—he couldn't get into because he's behind. I looked at the high schools in my zone, the one near me has both Bloods and Crips—if you don't know what those are, those are—those are street gangs. And so my stepson is in a private school, a private high school, where he has ten people per class, ten students per class. And I basically had no choice to do that.

So, and this is a full disclosure, I'm not one of those people who talks about the choice issue out of both sides of my face. You know, I

Excerpts from the transcript of a discussion The Century Foundation sponsored held at the National Press Club, Washington, D.C, September 27, 1999.

know I have the choice and I've exercised it. And, to some extent, our panelists will have to talk about why they think other people ought to be denied this choice....

ELLIOT MINCBERG: Governor Bush recommended something in Title I not so long ago. He said that if a school that's serving poor kids isn't doing its job in two years, you just give all the kids vouchers, give them $1,500 — which somehow he thinks is going to get them on a good life raft—and let them go their merry way.

But the proposal that is now up before Congress, supported by the administration, under Title I, would . . . say that if you have a school that is in trouble, you do a couple of things. First of all, you give the school extra resources to improve. Second of all, you give the school several years. And if the school hasn't improved, then you do two things that accomplish both the objectives that I've talked about.

First of all, you actually reconstitute the school—that's euphemism for saying fire the principal. Fire some of the teachers if you need to. Do what you need to do to shake it up, to put in the kinds of high expectations, Brent, that you talked about—to make sure that they're there, and to push them.

And second, you also give the kids some choice—not to take the money out of the system altogether, but to transfer to a higher performing public school with transportation and other mechanisms to be sure that the life raft works, as opposed to throwing them a life preserver and maybe hoping that they can swim through the rough shoals....

ADAM URBANSKI: I want to drive this home for you and zero in on your stepson-to-be, because you don't want to send him to what essentially you consider the lousy high school in New York City, and you say there are a lot of them, and that may be so. But, you and I also know that there are lots of wonderful high schools in District 2 in New York City—housing is not that expensive, the clientele is pretty much like the rest of the city. So it took a long time and it took leadership, but somebody proved what we all know is doable, and that is, in order to actually do right by the kids—particularly the kind of kids whom schools in this nation never served well—that you have other options than to opt out; that you can actually improve their schools on a mass scale. In District 2, children come from socioeconomic backgrounds not altogether different from the rest of the city, schools are outperforming many of the wealthy suburbs around them, and so the question is "Why?" Well, they took F.D.R.'s example and they did it in three stages: relief, recovery, and reform, so that we don't sacrifice the kids who are currently in school. And they have actually brought in programs, instructional strategies that are proven to work. And they have actually done what the National Commission on Teaching in America's Future later on reminded us in that report what matters most. They had made sure that every child is entitled and gets a knowledgeable, skilled teacher—caring teacher. In other words, they did what we rarely do in education, public or private, that is, they invested in R and D, in professional development of teachers to increase their knowledge and skills. And then, the state exams verified what we already noticed years before that, and that is that those kids—poor kids, all kids—are outperforming private school kids and are outperforming kids in much wealthier suburbs. So, what I would say is first of all, I agree with you to the extent that we ought not to ban children to low performing schools. Absolutely no question about it. Secondly, I would urge you to consider that if equity matters, and I believe there is no such thing as excellence without equity—excellence without equity is not excellence, it's privilege. I would rush no more to offer privilege to the kids that you are citing here by allowing them to opt out, and then forego equity if there is still any hope that we can actually improve schools for all kids. Because when you tell me, when you show me examples that public education or private schools can work for some kids, you're showing me nothing that I don't already know. I know we've got exceptions. I'm worried—for me the challenge is how do you make the exception into the norm....

CHRISTOPHER EDLEY: I have two—let me bring two perspectives to this—one, as someone who cares deeply about and spends a lot of his time working on matters of racial and ethnic justice, and the other is as a lawyer, or at least as a law professor.

The first perspective makes me burn with the kind of impatience that you just described. And, frankly, I think that I may be quite a bit less patient than Adam and Elliott in this respect. You know, most kids are eight years old only for about a year. And if they have a disastrous year in school, it's a year that's lost.

And it's very hard to make up. Perhaps my most fundamental concern about school reformers—left, right, middle, up, down, whatever; Democrat, Republican—a point that I've made in conversations with both the president and the vice president with respect to the administration's proposals, is that they're too patient for change, for dramatic change in our most troubled districts and our most struggling schools.

That there's a need for leaders who will identify with the burning impatience of the parents, who recognize the problems that their kids are facing, and of the teachers, who desperately want to improve the schools within which they work.

The civil rights—the lawyer hat on me makes me really want to avoid public policy by romantic anecdote.

We can't have a reform strategy that depends on the heroism of an Anthony Alvarado or of, you name it—of an Adam Urbanski for that matter. Nor can we have a public policy that depends on a mythology about free markets. What we need, it seems to me, is a structure of accountability geared to this accelerated pace that I am talking about, in which people are given the incentives to make the changes in directions, using strategies, that we have good reason to think that will produce results. In other words, I'm for testing, to see what's going on. But I would distinguish that from the kind of willy-nilly berserk, test-o-mania, neurosis, psychosis, that's been sweeping school reform, where the standards-based school reform movement is in danger of becoming a testing movement in which kids suffer consequences in their lives because they had the misfortune of having a poor school, a poor teacher, students with them in classrooms who were not motivated. The least powerful person in the system is the person we're most likely to hold accountable for failure, and that's wrong.

I also think that—again, thinking like a lawyer—we need to be prepared, as progressives, to challenge some assumptions about the structures within which schooling is delivered. I'm for public school choice.

Yes, let my kid get out of the failing public school. Help them get to a public school that is functioning. I'm for reconstitution, and not waiting two, three, four, five years to do it. I'm for looking back at what the track record has been and saying, "Sorry, you've had enough time." We need radical change, now. We need radical change, now.

I'm for wiping out this assumption that local school districts have sovereignty, and bleeding across the borders of political jurisdictions and bureaucratic jurisdictions so that students can go to schools in other school districts, and working out ways for multi-district, inter-district strategies. I think it will help with race. It will help with class. It will help with targeted resources. And I think it will help improve, if you will, this public choice market by giving parents and students more options, particularly if the transportation systems—this is a variable that Elliott mentioned, which is key—the transportation systems are in place to make the choice feasible.

I guess, before I subside, let me just make a basic point, because the other romantic ideal that we should not indulge is the notion that all the change is going to come from the bottom up; that parent driven and teacher driven change is all that's needed. I think I'm against reductionist solutions. It's not all bottom up and it's not all top down. But, especially for people in Washington, I think there is this danger, either of saying "We don't have to do anything but perhaps send out a few dollars, and all the good things will happen locally." I think that's just wrong.

Again, wearing my civil rights hat, I know that if you leave it to state and local politics, more often than not, the people about whom I care most will lose—will lose. That's the nature of politics.

We need strong federal engagement in the equity agenda in education. But it's got to be strong federal engagement that doesn't bow and scrape in front of the altar of states' rights and local autonomy, but that instead holds up an ideal of closing the disparities in educational attainment for poor kids, for children of color....

Adam Urbanski: Let me just say this. First of all, I want to say that I meant every word he said—(laughter). And secondly, what I like best about that perspective is that if it catches on, it will be an antidote to even a greater danger than the topic we're discussing, and the danger is polarizing this issue.

The polarization of this issue prevents us from having a thoughtful conversation. Now, I know and I've experienced the effects of shock value. I think that sometimes we have to be shocked into a real conversation. But then, after the shock, I think we have to somehow avoid this polarizing of the issue, because the answer is not in either extreme.

The answer has to be thoughtful and sort of a medley of considerations. It's not a question of choice or no choice, it's a question of more choice. And at least most of us can find common ground on public school choice. And we can argue about why limit it to that for now, or to what extent it need not be limited.

It's not a question of public versus private. In your packets, there is at least some drivel—I mean some writing by me—about how we could actually make public schools more like private, and the system more like that, without privatizing public schools.

So I think it would be more productive to recognize the complexity of the issue and to find common ground so that we can quickly move to solutions rather than spend another decade arguing about ideology and about which extreme is correct and which one is not.

Elliot Mincberg: Let me just add one other thing, because I know we want to throw this open fairly soon as well. It really was a caricature—and I know you were doing it on purpose—to suggest that all we are interested in was structural engineering on the Titanic, because I think all of us are impatient, as Chris put it, and want to have solutions now. And the kinds of things we're talking about—a program like SAGE that works not in five years but in one year to improve a public school—that the parents that we work with in Milwaukee demanded from their legislature.

Or as people have talked about, the option to provide choice within a public school system to be sure, therefore, that the places to which kids choose (a), will take them and (b), will be accountable in a way that private schools will not be are things that can and should work now.

But I am grateful, believe it or not, to those that have proposed vouchers, because what they have done is to cause this kind of session to take place, and to make sure that everybody from the teachers union to People For [the American Way], to civil rights advocates are being forced to say what will work—what will work in a few years, and what will work now to give opportunity to the kids that you're talking about.

Adam Urbanski: I would seek to equalize resources by prohibiting any urban district from remaining self-contained—that is, by making metropolitan school systems a requirement so that those who are now avoiding our children would have to realize that they need to be part of the solution.

Without that, I think you're rearranging things that already exist, and what you're doing is not reform but remodeling of a hopeless situation.

Secondly, I would support full public school choice. Full. Now that you've leveled the ground—the playing-field—now, full public school choice, because I'll tell you, the parents of the children in Pittsford, New York, outside of Rochester, where I live, if we had full choice—public school choice—they would never permit any school to be in a condition that they are now in a city, for fear that their child might end up in it.

Third, I would make public schools more like private without privatizing them. That means school–family compacts—two-way choice, just like private schools have now. That means logical consequences in market sensitivity. I am in favor of that. I would make public schools more like private without privatizing them.

The People's Choice for Schools

Richard D. Kahlenberg

Aides to President-elect George W. Bush have indicated that he will push education policy early in the new administration as a way of building bridges. If Bush wants the education debate to help unite the country, he should begin by dropping his plan for private school vouchers and endorsing instead a policy of greater public school choice that draws on the best arguments of both sides of the voucher debate.

Although the presidential election results could be stood on a knife's edge, the electorate's verdict on private school vouchers was resounding. Voucher initiatives in Michigan and California were rejected by roughly 70 percent of voters. Nationally, exit polls found that by a 78–15 percent margin, voters preferred programs to fix public schools over private school voucher plans. At the same time, voters elected a Congress and a president supportive of vouchers. This combination creates a unique opportunity for voucher opponents and supporters to converge around a third alternative: public school vouchers.

Proponents of vouchers are right in their critique of the current education system: It's unfair that poor children whose families can't afford neighborhoods with good public schools or private school tuition, are forced to attend terrible schools in areas where poverty is concentrated. They are right to say it's intolerable to ask parents to wait a generation to see whether public school reform succeeds. And they're right to cite the hypocrisy of those who defend the status quo—some members of Congress and teachers among others—but who would never send their own children to certain public schools.

But none of that adds up to an argument for giving up on public schools and entertaining the risks associated with voucher schemes.

Originally published as "The People's Choice for Schools," *Washington Post*, December 15, 2000.

We already have evidence, from this country and others, that no matter how bad the current education system is, it can get worse under a system of private school vouchers.

The biggest threat to equal educational opportunity and to overall school quality today is the economic segregation of schools. Students who attend school with large numbers of poor children are likely to be educated in a setting where there are fewer financial resources, where peers are less likely to be highly motivated, and where parents are less likely to be active in the school. These students are more likely to be taught a watered-down curriculum, to experience high levels of student disorder, and to be taught by unprepared teachers than are students in schools with largely middle-class populations.

There is considerable evidence that private school vouchers only make matters worse. In Sweden, a voucher experiment instituted in 1992 exacerbated ethnic and economic segregation as Swedish-origin children and well-off immigrant children abandoned low-income immigrant schools. Likewise, in Chile, according to Stanford professor Martin Carnoy's study, a voucher program adopted in 1980 resulted in the flight of middle- and upper-class families to private schools. Recent research by Edward Fiske and Helen Ladd in New Zealand confirms these earlier findings.

The pattern is likely to be replicated in the United States. Under voucher schemes, choice is given not to parents but to schools. Because private schools can be selective—and because achievement and behavior correlate with socioeconomic status—unregulated private choice is likely to cream off the most advantaged and motivated public school students, leaving the least motivated behind and in worse shape than ever.

Across class lines, vouchers are likely to underline and harden religious and racial differences. In the Netherlands, one study found that public support for separate religiously affiliated schools has "reinforced the religious segmentation within society."

Finally, because private schools are not accountable in the way public schools are, there is no guarantee they will promote the democratic values that are a central part of the public school curriculum. Unregulated private schools can be segregated academies that promote with public funds racial supremacy or black separatism or other doctrines.

None of this argues for the gradualist public school reform approach that is dominant among progressives: reducing class size, increasing teacher training, raising standards and calling it a day. The *Post* was right to note in a recent editorial that "inner-city school reform has been going on for just about as long as inner-city school failure." The answer lies in closing failing schools and providing students with vouchers to attend better, middle-class, public schools of their choice. In a nation where the vast majority of students come from middle-class homes, public school choice can, if properly structured, give every child a chance to attend a middle-class school. In order for it to be fully successful, students at failing city schools must be given access to suburban public schools located within a reasonable distance. In the case of D.C. students, federal funds could provide incentives for nearby Virginia and Maryland schools to admit manageable numbers of city students, modeled after successful city–suburban programs in Hartford, Boston and St. Louis.

Public school choice does not divide the electorate as vouchers do; some 70 to 80 percent of Americans consistently support greater public school choice. And because roughly 90 percent of students attend public schools, a system of public school choice offers a far more realistic opportunity for genuine choice than do private-school voucher schemes.

For the new administration, backing public school vouchers would constitute a potent symbol of bipartisanship and an excellent way to make progress on the goal of leaving no child behind.

8.

Public School Choice: Student Achievement, Integration, Democracy, and Public Support

Equitable Public School Choice

Richard D. Kahlenberg

The controlled choice, or conditional choice, strategy was formulated by Professors Charles Willie, of Harvard University, and Michael Alves, of Brown.[1] Under existing controlled choice plans, rather than assigning students to neighborhood schools, which tend to reflect stratified residential patterns, school districts allow parents and students to choose the public school they would like to attend within a given geographical region; no guarantees are made; districts then honor these choices in a way that promotes racial integration. Although controlled choice has traditionally been designed to promote racial balance, it can easily be modified to achieve economic balancing through what might be called common school choice.

Under most controlled choice plans, families provide a first, second, and third choice of schools at the levels of kindergarten, sixth, and ninth grades. Information and outreach programs attempt to ensure

---

Excerpts from Richard D. Kahlenberg, *All Together Now: Creating Middle-Class Schools through Public School Choice*, A Century Foundation Book (Washington, D.C.: Brookings Institution Press, 2001).

that parents are well informed. A central officer makes the decisions, so that individual schools cannot pick those promising students they believe will be easiest to teach. The process of assignment must be objective and shielded from political influence.[2]

Sensible accommodations are made to give preference to students who live within a short walk to the school; in the Cambridge, Massachusetts, controlled choice plan, for example, students within one-eighth of a mile are given preference. Similarly, once a child is admitted to a school, a younger sibling should be given preference so that families are not divided. Plans can be phased in gradually, grandfathering existing student placements to minimize disruption. Variations on the controlled choice plan are possible (for example, preferred choice, under which parents are guaranteed the neighborhood school as a fallback), though they offer less promise for integration.[3]

Controlled choice is designed to maximize parental satisfaction. Before plans are implemented, families are surveyed to see what kinds of choices they would like for their children.[4] If the survey finds that 40 percent of parents want a highly disciplined environment with uniforms, and only 10 percent want a French immersion school, then the makeup of the choices should reflect that general preference. For parents who say they believe it is too early for their children to specialize, options for "regular" schools should be made available. Respect for parent choice and preference continues after the initial decisions are made in the "signatures" that attach to various schools. Schools that are undersubscribed year after year will be closed down or reconstituted. Schools that are continually oversubscribed and deemed successful will be replicated.

Controlled choice has been used in about one in twenty districts nationwide, including several cities in Massachusetts (Boston, Brockton, Cambridge, Chelsea, Fall River, Holyoke, Lawrence, Lowell, Northampton, Salem, Somerville, and Springfield) as well as Seattle, Washington; Milwaukee, Wisconsin; Little Rock, Arkansas; San Jose, California; Indianapolis, Indiana; Montclair, New Jersey; White Plains, New York; Yonkers, New York; Buffalo, New York; East Harlem, New York; Glendale, California; St. Lucie County, Florida; Fort Meyers, Florida; LaGrange, Georgia; Rockford, Illinois; Troup County, Georgia; Pawtucket, Rhode Island; and Mobile, Alabama.[5] In the 1990s, 18 percent of Massachusetts students attended school in districts with controlled choice, and if other school systems with active public choice are included, the figure rises to 25 percent. Controlled choice has bipartisan support, and the Cambridge controlled choice plan was lauded by President George Bush, his secretary of education, William Bennett, and the conservative Manhattan Institute. In only a few cities has the controlled choice mechanism run into serious political trouble. Controlled choice based on race has come under legal attack recently, but the economic version advocated here currently faces no such legal difficulty.[6]

Studies find that in public schools of choice, attendance rates are generally higher and dropout rates are lower. Achievement gains have followed the adoption of controlled public school choice—or a modified version of controlled choice—in a number of cities, including Cambridge, Montclair, Buffalo, and Lowell.[7] Controlled choice combines the best elements of—and improves upon—three alternative models of school assignment: compulsory assignment (through busing or by residence), uncontrolled choice, and magnet schools.

Controlled choice versus compulsory assignment. Controlled choice offers several advantages over traditional compulsory assignment schemes that either assign students based on residence or bus them based on a combination of residence and race. Whereas in the early days of desegregation, resistance was so obdurate that "choice" was usually an excuse for avoiding integration, today there is something of a policy consensus that choice should be part of the desegregation effort, and since 1981 most desegregation plans have used some element of choice.[8]

Choice fundamentally adds a right rather than takes one away. Whereas desegregation by forced busing made parents feel impotent—pawns in a system run by others—controlled choice gives them a new voice. We already have choice for those who can afford to buy into good neighborhoods or to choose private schools, but a system of public school choice greatly enlarges the circle of people who can exercise that choice. "The debate is not whether we'll have education choice," says Joe Nathan; it is, rather, "whether state and local governments will expand educational choice to low- and moderate-income people." In this way, public school choice plans combine greater freedom with greater equity. Public school choice, the AFT's Bella Rosenberg writes, attempts to create a system in which "no child [will] be trapped in a bad or poor neighborhood school simply because of the economic or social circumstances of his parents."

Unlike busing for racial balance, public choice has intrinsic educational merit in that it allows different schools to emphasize different pedagogical approaches or curricular themes among which parents can choose, based on the individual needs of their children. Students who will languish in a regular school might flourish in a Comer school, a small school, a Montessori school, an international-baccalaureate school, a Dewey-inspired progressive school, a back-to-basics school, a classical-studies school (Mortimer Adler), a multiple-intelligence school (Howard Gardner), a gifted and talented school, a future-studies school, an international-studies school, a whole-language school, a bilingual school, or a school specializing in the arts, science, business, or computers.[9] Parents can choose between an E. D. Hirsch–style "core-knowledge" school, which emphasizes coverage of broad swaths of academic material, or a Theodore Sizer–style "essential school," which emphasizes in-depth knowledge about a much smaller number of topics. Indeed, choice has such independent educational merit that it is often advocated in school districts in which desegregation is not an issue. Some evidence suggests that public school choice raises student achievement.[10]

So too, choice allows for a better correspondence between teachers and school philosophies of education. Many educators believe it is important for teachers to agree with a principal on their school's educational philosophy in order to be part of an effective team. As Evan Clinchy and Frances Kolb note, however, teachers are often assigned to "neighborhood schools on the basis of existing vacancies and seniority, whether or not they agree with the particular school's philosophy and educational practices."[11] A system of controlled choice allows both students and teachers to be matched individually with educational beliefs. Everyone benefits when that matching occurs.

Choice also spurs competition and puts pressure on administrators to improve bad schools. Under busing or neighborhood assignment, bad schools are assured a steady stream of students. Under choice, a school that fails, year after year, to provide a hospitable learning environment—even with a new economic mix of students—may be shut down by the school board. Studies find that public school choice results in greater performance by both the choice schools and the remaining neighborhood schools because bureaucracies become more responsive to the need for change.[12]

Of course, for the market analogy to work there must be consequences for schools that perform poorly. Severely underchosen schools should be closed and the buildings used to house "franchises" of the overchosen schools. Willie and Alves recommend that undersubscribed schools be given three years to improve, and in several cities that use controlled choice, failing schools have been closed.[13] Under normal circumstances, districts are hesitant to close failing schools because principals can blame high poverty rates for poor performance. Controlled choice takes away this excuse. Because properly implemented controlled choice plans will put large numbers of middle-class parents in all schools, where they will exert pressure to ensure that all schools are serving children, remaining differences in quality will truly be the fault of the school. Unlike busing or residential assignment, choice provides tangible evidence of a school's success: parents who are displeased with a school's performance can "vote" the school out of existence.

Controlled choice has also been found to spur parental involvement. It has long been known that parents who choose private schools are more active, though some have discounted this greater involvement because private school parents are a self-selected motivated group who, having plunked down their own money, are likely to want to monitor their investments. Public school choice is also associated with greater parental involvement. The process of choosing a school, writes Deborah Meier, "creates bonds between parents, teachers, and students that are in themselves important."[14] In addition, parents may feel a greater incentive to be involved because they believe that choice gives them greater leverage with school authorities. Some parents may feel "greater affiliation" with a chosen school because they "approve" of its focus. Empirical studies in Minneapolis, Alum Rock (California), Boston, Milwaukee, New York, and New Jersey have found that parental involvement increased after the adoption of school choice.[15] Parents feel especially empowered when school officials, in setting up a controlled choice plan, survey parents in advance about the kinds of pedagogy and subject specialties the parents want.[16]

Under controlled choice parents cannot avoid desegregation by moving to a different neighborhood within the school district. When school desegregation is accomplished by redrawing boundary lines, parents have the option of moving—sometimes only across the street—so that their children can attend less integrated schools. Under Supreme Court decisions, courts are powerless to address changing demographic patterns, and schools are unlikely to voluntarily redraw boundaries on an annual basis to maintain racially balanced schools.[17] When an entire district is under controlled choice, residential location within the district makes no difference. This advantage holds even outside the desegregation arena: choice is more responsive to general shifts in population that leave a neighborhood school system with some schools overcrowded and others underutilized. Similarly, controlled choice allows a student who moves within the district to remain in his or her school, reducing disruption to the child's education as well as to the school.[18]

While the "control" in controlled choice means that some families' choices may be constrained in order to implement the integration goal, the evidence suggests that in practice, only rarely are children assigned to schools they do not want to attend in order to satisfy integration requirements. In any event, in comparison with the prevailing system of neighborhood assignment, controlled choice represents a large net increase in parental choice.

The degree to which parental choice and socioeconomic integration conflict depends on the prevalence of three phenomena. First, to what degree do parents, even when given a choice, prefer the neighborhood school for reasons of convenience? Because neighborhood schools tend to reflect economic and racial residential segregation, the preference for neighborhood schools will mean that poor children may trend toward schools in poor neighborhoods and rich children to schools in rich neighborhoods. Second, to what degree, in the aggregate, do whites and blacks and rich and poor tend to prefer different types of schools? If parents' choices of pedagogical approaches sort out roughly by class—with rich parents preferring progressive education and language immersion and poor parents preferring back-to-basics schools and schools stressing obedience—then choice may result in economic stratification independent of neighborhood. Third, to what degree will the desire of families to aggregate by race undercut the effort to integrate by class, given the overlap between the two? If these three phenomena are potent, then the goal of economic balance will strongly conflict with choice. The evidence suggests, however, that a well-run system of controlled choice can normally honor both choice and integration.

For one thing, there is substantial evidence that sufficient numbers of parents will choose a school other than the neighborhood school. Many parents are willing to send their children to distant magnet schools with the promise of a better educational fit for their children—indeed, many magnets have long waiting lists; similarly, more than 70 percent of charter schools have more applicants than they can accommodate.[19] Increasingly, in some school districts, parents are so desperate to move their children out of inferior neighborhood schools that they will commit fraud and lie about residency to get their children into better suburban schools. In Boston, many minority students are willing to take long bus rides to attend suburban schools; under the voluntary Metropolitan Council for Educational Opportunity (Metco) program, which has a waiting list of seven thousand students (twice the size of the current program), some 25 percent of Metco parents register their children before the child's first birthday. The same is true of similar programs in Hartford, Rochester, Chicago, and Louisville.[20]

The popularity of vouchers among low-income and African American communities in particular suggests that where better education is available, families will be willing to travel beyond the neighborhood school. When a philanthropist contributed money for a thousand scholarships for Washington, D.C., students to attend private schools, more than seventy-five hundred students—about 10 percent of the public school enrollment—applied. When Cleveland began its publicly funded voucher program for two thousand students, some six thousand families signed up. In 1999, philanthropists Theodore Forstmann and John Walton offered forty thousand private scholarships for poor students in kindergarten through eighth grade; more than a million students applied, including 44 percent of all eligible students in Baltimore.[21]

In 1998, a Public Agenda poll found that 60 percent of black parents would "switch their kids from public to private school if money were not an obstacle," suggesting that they are not wedded to neighborhood public schools when superior offerings are realistically available. Most significantly, a 1996 Gallup/*Phi Delta Kappan* poll found that 45 percent of all parents would choose schools outside of their neighborhoods for their children if given the chance.[22]

In areas in which controlled choice has been implemented and parents are accustomed to the concept, the numbers choosing nonneighborhood schools can be even higher. Alves has found that under Cambridge's controlled choice plan, 60–65 percent chose a school other than the neighborhood school; in Boston, 45 percent initially chose nonneighborhood schools, and the percentage later climbed to 57 percent. According to Boston school committee chair Bob Gittens, a recent study has found that "people are choosing schools that may not be the closest in terms of distance . . . [based on the school's] perceived quality."[23] In Montclair, New Jersey, another controlled choice district, the majority of families choose nonneighborhood schools. Even if small numbers of parents—as low as 15 percent—choose nonneighborhood schools, the schools could be significantly more integrated than under a system of residential assignment.[24]

For another, the evidence suggests that parental tastes in pedagogy do not neatly break down along economic and racial lines. Although some early studies found that the poor trended toward structured programs and the wealthy toward unstructured programs, more recent hard evidence suggests broad similarities.[25] In Cambridge's controlled choice plan, racial groups did not vary in their choices. Alves and Willie have found that "the pattern of school choice is remarkably similar for both majority and minority parents, thereby minimizing mandatory assignments due to race"; the same was true in Boston and in Lowell, Massachusetts. Charles Glenn notes that desegregation succeeded in Springfield and Worcester, Massachusetts, because "black and Hispanic and white parents were roughly the same" in their pedagogical preferences.[26]

Finally, evidence suggests that today most Americans put a higher premium on the quality of education than on the racial makeup of the student body. Although African Americans may have legitimate reasons to aggregate, polls suggest that most blacks support residential integration; only one-fifth wish to live in all-black areas. Whereas in 1964, 62 percent of blacks wanted to live in "mostly black" neighborhoods and only 4 percent in "mostly white" neighborhoods, today, large majorities of blacks wish to live in integrated neighborhoods. In a survey of ghetto residents in Chicago in the late 1980s, only 23 percent said that if given the option to move they would prefer to stay in their own neighborhood. Massey and Denton have found that the majority of blacks want to live in neighborhoods that are roughly half white and half black, and 95 percent are willing to live with a 15 percent black population. In a Detroit study, parents ranked "safety" and supportive "values" as most important considerations in their children's schools; the lowest rank was given to schooling with children whose parents have "educational and occupational backgrounds similar to me." Meanwhile, among whites, the percentage who said they would move if a black moved into the neighborhood dropped from 44 percent in 1958 to 1 percent in 1998.[27]

If only limited numbers of blacks and whites value aggregation over education, it is even less likely that the poor will want to aggregate. For one thing, from an academic standpoint, economic integration is in the self-interest of the poor who will do better; racial integration does not in itself benefit blacks academically. For another, although there are legitimate reasons that an ethnic group may wish to aggregate (to promote an ethnic culture, for example), the poor do not have a specific culture they wish to preserve.

Two additional steps can be taken to reconcile choice and integration. First, to the extent that preimplementation parent surveys reveal any socioeconomic leanings toward certain programs (for example, wealthier parents trending toward progressive or alternative schooling), the district can place those progressive programs in formerly blue-collar neighborhood schools so that the tendency of some to prefer neighborhood schools counteracts the pedagogical preference. In this way, middle-class and working-class parents are more likely to divide their choices between schools, with some favoring neighborhood and others opting for a preferred pedagogy. This strategy has proven highly successful in Montclair, where 95 percent of students receive their first choice and schools are nicely balanced by race and by socioeconomic status.[28]

Similarly, because part of the reason certain schools may be underchosen will have to do with the school's past reputation, officials can place the most popular pedagogical approaches or subject areas (as revealed in the parent survey) in the previously stigmatized school. Under controlled choice, a new influx of middle-class families will put pressure on schools to improve. If this does not work, severely underchosen schools should be closed and reopened with a clean slate of faculty and leadership.

A second mechanism, which maximizes choice but maintains basic integration, allows schools to employ a band or range of socioeconomic makeup rather than a rigid number. Although the goal might be 33 percent FARM-eligible students in every school, schools might be permitted to fall within a range of, for example, 15–45 percent FARM eligible, to accommodate choice. Court orders involving racial desegregation have typically used a guideline of plus or minus 15 percent.[29]

Taking these facts together, the number of students in controlled choice districts who are assigned to schools not of their choice is very small. Boston and Cambridge boast placement in first-, second-, or third-choice schools at around the 90 percent level—a rate replicated in other jurisdictions using controlled choice, like St. Lucie County, Florida; Lowell, Massachusetts; Montclair, New Jersey; and White Plains, New York.[30] Moreover, most of those who do not receive their first choice are turned down because of overall space limitations having nothing to do with racial balance. Glenn notes that in 1990, only 1.7 percent of students assigned to Boston schools (238 of 14,041 first-, sixth-, and ninth-graders) "were either denied a place or assigned involuntarily to a place that another student was denied in order to meet the requirements of desegregation." In a 1995 Bain and Company survey, 80 percent of parents said they were satisfied with controlled choice, and 72 percent said they preferred having a choice to assignment based on neighborhood schools.[31]

Although some critics fixate on the 1.7 percent whose choice is constrained by integration goals, the movement from neighborhood schools to controlled choice represents an enormous expansion of choice, particularly for the poor. Today, private school choice is still largely the province of the well-to-do; families making less than $15,000 a year are five times less likely to choose private schools as those making more than $50,000; and those with no education beyond high school are eight times less likely to choose private schools as those with graduate degrees.[32] Among those assigned to public schools, the poor are almost twice as likely to be assigned to schools they did not choose even indirectly, through residential choice. By contrast, those with little education and income are twice as likely as the wealthy to use public school choice.[33]

Researchers estimate that roughly 36 percent of all elementary and secondary schoolchildren attend neighborhood schools consciously chosen by their parents in deciding where to reside—and that wealthier families are much more likely to have done so. For many families, choosing a residence based on school district is a luxury; as Alves expresses it, "The priority of the family is they've got to find a decent place to live that they can afford." For the poor, assignment to unpopular neighborhood schools is a fact of life. As a practical matter, Glenn notes, poor and working-class people are effectively denied what is considered by the Universal Declaration of Human Rights (1948) a "right to choose the kind of education that shall be given to their children."[34]

It is ironic, Glenn notes elsewhere, that in moving from assigned schools to controlled choice, critics focus on the small amount of control rather than the enormous flowering of freedom. "An inevitable cost of freedom is to experience remaining constraint as galling," he writes. "So long as children are simply assigned to school involuntarily on the basis of where they live, of course, the issue of disappointment does not arise."[35] Moving to controlled choice means that 90 percent get one of their top choices—as opposed to the 36 percent who today choose a neighborhood school—and it is unreasonable to focus on the 10 percent who fail to have their choice honored rather than the majority who realize a net gain in choice.

Because choice redistributes opportunity, the chance of each child is equal to that of every other and is not contingent upon a parent's ability to pay. Whereas affluent families today can purchase a 100 percent lock on a particular school, and many poor families effectively have no choice, under controlled choice everyone has a 90 percent chance for basic satisfaction. Controlled choice provides an overall net increase in choice and a fairer distribution of choice, as well. Choice uses equality to increase freedom for the poor, while continuing to allow the middle class a variety of common school choices; in this way, equality becomes a source of freedom, not its enemy.[36]

Controlled versus uncontrolled choice. If it is true that choice and integration do not normally conflict in controlled choice plans, then why not just use uncontrolled choice? Why the need for "control"? The problem is that uncontrolled choice can actually produce more, not less, segregation. Like electricity, Joe Nathan notes, public school choice is "a powerful tool capable of producing helpful or harmful effects, depending on its use."[37] Four elements of controlled choice plans are crucial to ensuring that plans promote, rather than undercut, socioeconomic integration.

First, choice must be controlled to avoid the "prisoner's dilemma" issue—that people act based in part on how they think others will act. If race and economic status are not considered, patterns of racial and economic segregation may be hard to break. Traditionally, middle-class parents, when considering neighborhoods and visiting schools, ask about test scores, which are given in absolute terms, rather than as the value added by a school.[38] Because socioeconomic status is linked to test scores, those schools that had middle-class populations in the past are likely under uncontrolled choice to draw disproportionate numbers of highly informed middle-class parents, while low-income schools will attract few middle-class families, and the cycle will continue.[39] If affluent parents have no guarantee that the new computer-centered school located in a tough neighborhood will have a predominantly middle-class student body, they may choose conservatively, based on what schools middle-class children have attended in the past, rather than based on the school theme.

This has been the experience in places like Kansas City and Prince George's County, where magnet schools, despite the expenditure of extra money, were unable to attract middle-class white students. These districts face a chicken-and-egg problem: in order to attract middle-class students, the key prerequisite is not so much the expenditure of money—many central cities already outspend suburban areas—as it is a critical mass of other middle-class children.[40] But who will go first? Similarly, a poor black family may like the back-to-basics emphasis in a school found in an affluent white neighborhood but hesitate to apply because the parents do not want their child to be isolated as the only student of color in his or her class.

In either case, parents do not have true choice in pedagogy. With controlled choice, on the other hand, the fear of being an economic or racial "pioneer" is eliminated from the equation. Christopher Jencks notes that "if the traditions and distinctive identity of a school depend not on the character of the student body but on the special objectives and methods of the staff, middle-class parents who approve of these objectives and methods will often send their children despite the presence of poorer classmates." Because schools will develop distinct themes or pedagogical strategies and all schools will have a similar economic makeup, families will choose schools based on an emphasis on French, or a back-to-basics approach, or the fact that the school provides an after-school program, rather than the anticipated social class of the students.[41]

The second crucial feature of controlled choice plans is that they require every family to choose a school, even if their choice is the neighborhood school. There is mounting evidence that when parents must take the initiative to choose, unregulated and poorly designed public school choice plans can actually exacerbate rather than alleviate concentrations of race and class.[42] The key problem, studies show, is that the least educated parents are least likely to avail themselves of choice, and the most aggressive parents, predominantly middle class and highly educated, dominate the system. This is particularly true when parents gain an edge by camping out all night to be first in line. Richard Elmore and Bruce Fuller conclude that "a large part of the stratification problem seems to result from parents and students who simply do not choose, rather than from differing preferences among those who do choose. That is, once parents and students make the decision to choose and actively exploit the opportunities that decision presents, they seem to have preferences that are remarkably similar across race and social class."[43]

Controlled choice protects against that possibility by requiring people to make a choice of schools. Because no family is guaranteed its neighborhood school, everyone has incentive to choose. Business recognizes that for the competitive aspects of choice to be fully realized, all parents must be required to choose, and the National Alliance of Business has endorsed "mandatory choice." Well-designed controlled choice plans also provide for mail-in registration so that there is no advantage to being first in line.[44]

Third, controlled choice plans strictly limit the number of schools that can handpick students, whereas uncontrolled choice plans—including voucher schemes—generally do not. In principle, there is a place for a small number of selective public high schools—such as Thomas Jefferson in Virginia, Stuyvesant in New York, or Boston Latin—and these schools should not be required to admit a certain percentage of students from disadvantaged backgrounds.[45] Poor children can earn their way into these elite public schools through hard work; and indeed, such schools can provide an escape from poverty for hardworking poor students. Many elite public schools—Scarsdale, or New Trier—tend to be based on the wealth of parents, but a school such as Bronx High School of Science is quite different.

That having been said, controlled choice plans should strictly limit the number of public schools that use admissions tests. If the number of such public academies were to proliferate, they could be used as a way to avoid the economic desegregation plan of a district. The competitive-school loophole to the general economic integration plan must remain small, or it will swallow the rule.

Particularly as schools become more publicly accountable, those schools with a choice of students will have a powerful incentive to pick the brightest ones. As Natriello and colleagues note, "There are only two ways to get high-achieving students: recruit them, or transform low achievers into high achievers. Currently it is easier to recruit high achievers than to create them." If schools choose students, those schools that begin as popular will grow even more so; schools that begin as less desirable will grow more so, as well. Even where schools are not permitted to choose students, schools that are not subject to controlled choice can find ways to subtly discourage students who are likely to drag down scores from applying or to encourage low-scoring students to drop out.[46]

Fourth, controlled choice plans pay transportation costs and offer information outreach; uncontrolled choice plans often do not and can thereby effectively exclude participation of the poor. In Richmond, California, for example, a plan allowing students to choose from forty-five schools saw only forty-one hundred of thirty-one thousand students choose a nonneighborhood school and actually exacerbated racial segregation, in part because the plan required parents of elementary schoolchildren to pay their own transportation costs. In the case of city-to-suburb choice plans, experience shows low levels of participation among poor minorities in districts that required parents to pay part of their transportation costs (Minneapolis and St. Paul) but much greater participation where the state paid for transportation (St. Louis and Milwaukee). The transportation costs are not unmanageable: according to a 1994 Department of Education study, 72 percent of school systems offering elementary transfer choice provide free transportation, as do 57 percent for middle schools and 48 percent for high schools.[47]

Well-informed choice can be encouraged by giving notice on television, mailing out letters clearly explaining the choice system, and making the choice forms easy to return. Outreach to poor parents was critical to the success of New York City's District Four program.[48]

Controlled choice versus magnet schools. Controlled choice also offers a better approach than magnetization of a few schools within a district. Magnets aspire to contribute to integration by admitting students from many neighborhoods and using a distinctive curriculum or form of instruction to draw in a racially balanced population. Magnets also create new forms of unfairness, however, and are inherently limited in their reach.

First, magnet schools create new inequities because they typically receive more funding than the regular schools (to provide, for example, better scientific equipment). On average, magnet schools spend 10–12 percent more for each pupil than other schools, and some magnets spend as much as double the average amount. Nicholas Lemann asks, "Is it fair for school districts to operate two classes of schools, one plainly better than the other?" In 1998, Public Agenda's focus groups found some dissatisfaction with magnets. "'In order to get the higher-income white kids into the projects, they have a magnet school,' began an African American parent in Raleigh. 'I'm ticked because my son wasn't allowed to go to that school. This school has everything; I have to drive past it every day. It makes my blood boil.'" Another black parent commented, "Why not make all the schools like that?"[49]

Second, not only do magnet schools receive more money, they also often cream off the best students, teachers, and parents. Because magnets normally rely on the motivation of parents to apply—and because balancing is based on race, not class—they tend to attract middle-class whites and the most advantaged blacks. Many disadvantaged families simply will not apply at all. One study of magnet programs in Philadelphia and Houston found that the policies "have reduced racial segregation but have increased the economic segregation of students" by drawing high-status students away from low-income schools. A recent study of magnet schools in St. Louis and Cincinnati has similarly found that "social class creaming" was prevalent. Nationally, low-income students are underrepresented in magnet schools, according to the Department of Education. "Magnet schools have neatly substituted class for race or neighborhood," notes Lemann, "as the governing principle of a segregated school system."[50]

In the case of selective magnet schools, this problem is especially acute: schools admit the students who are the easiest to teach, who also tend to be the most affluent. According to studies, two-thirds of magnet schools are selective "by some admissions criteria," and 15 percent are highly selective, using test scores. In the case of secondary magnet schools, more than half use admissions tests. Some selective magnets reject as many as 95 percent of applicants. In addition, some magnet schools are free to expel students who do not perform at prescribed levels, a power conventional public schools lack. Extra funding goes to the most advantaged students—a reversal of the principle of funding by need. As a result, Charles Glenn notes, "there is a widening gap between students who grab the brass ring—who get into selective magnets—and those who don't." Magnets also often attract the very best teachers, and they can siphon off the most active parents, those who would otherwise push for needed change in less successful schools.[51]

Third, in certain districts, while the magnet schools themselves might be racially integrated, they often leave other schools more racially segregated. Particularly in high-minority districts, packing the few whites into magnets (to create an even racial mix in schools) can leave the rest of the schools all black.[52] This creates dissatisfaction among those in nonmagnet schools and severely limits the reach of integration efforts.

Fourth, because magnets are more expensive, their number is by necessity limited, and large numbers of students are rejected and are consigned to traditional public schools with inferior resources. One study finds that magnet schools serve an average of 5.2 percent of students. For desegregation purposes, Jennifer Hochschild writes, "magnets are better characterized as a drop in the bucket than a cure for what ails us." Even in large urban districts, where magnet schools have taken greatest hold, only 20 percent of students attend magnets, the remaining 80 percent attending the other nonmagnet schools.[53]

Controlled choice, by contrast, requires everyone to choose, "magnetizes" all schools, eliminates the double standard, and maximizes the chances that families will receive their top choice of education. Whereas magnet schools reject large numbers of applicants, in school districts that use controlled choice, as noted, as many as 90 percent of families receive one of their first choices. Controlled choice has proved more popular in some communities because it maintains the benefits of choice inherent in the magnet approach without creating a two-tier system. Similarly, whereas magnet schools cream off the best parents, under controlled choice, middle-class parents may be assigned to any school, placing pressure on inferior schools to improve or die.[54]

Controlled choice does adopt the insights of the magnet school approach—that the reputation of a school is an enduring thing and that middle-class parents will need incentives to send their children to schools in poor neighborhoods that were, under the old regime, educationally inferior. Instead of creating new inequities through extreme variations in spending, however, controlled choice attracts middle-class parents with the promise of a middle-class environment and other carrots—for example, placing the most popular curriculum in a previously inferior school. In addition, the most creative and well-respected principals can be placed in the former high-poverty schools as a way of attracting good teachers and middle-class families.[55] (The additional incentives required to lure middle-class children across district lines are discussed momentarily.) All this is meant to provide equality: the idea is that underchosen and unpopular schools should get extra help, not as a way of creating a new school that is twice as good as all the others but as a way of creating equality—much as losing athletic teams get the first pick of new talent in the next year's draft.

ELIMINATING POVERTY CONCENTRATIONS THROUGH PUBLIC SCHOOL CHOICE

THE CENTURY FOUNDATION TASK FORCE ON THE COMMON SCHOOL

Nearly forty years ago, Alabama Governor George Wallace declared in his inaugural address, "Segregation today, segregation tomorrow, segregation forever." Today, almost no American would embrace what was once the reigning ethos, but the everyday reality lived by millions of schoolchildren is not too far from Wallace's vision. No longer segregated by law, our nation's schools are increasingly segregated in fact—both by race and ethnicity and, increasingly, by economic class. Our nation made great strides to eradicate segregated schooling from the early 1970s to the mid-1980s, but since then we have seen increasing racial and economic segregation, and almost no one—from either political party—has articulated a clear plan for addressing this disastrous trend.

The past twenty years have seen an explosion of education policy debates, over issues ranging from raising academic standards to lowering class size; from improving teacher training to promoting afterschool programs. But current discussions largely ignore the central source of school inequality: segregation by class and race. All of history suggests that separate schools, particularly for poor and middle-class children, are inherently unequal. A child growing up in a poor family has reduced life chances, but attending a school with large numbers of low-income classmates poses a second, independent strike against him or her. While some look at the stubborn link between poverty and achievement and conclude that failure is inevitable, the members of

---

Excerpts from *Divided We Fail: Coming Together through Public School Choice: The Report of The Century Foundation Task Force on the Common School* (New York: Century Foundation Press, 2002).

this Task Force believe that poor children, given the right environment in school, can achieve at very high levels.

There exists today a solid consensus among researchers that school segregation perpetuates failure, and an equally durable consensus among politicians that nothing much can be done about it. Education reformers take as a given that schools will reflect residential segregation by class and race and therefore any solutions are narrowly conceived to make separate schools more equal. We believe that this approach is seriously flawed.

We fully recognize that the existing segregation of schools by class and race is not an accident, but is in some measure a reflection of political power. "Busing," defined as compulsory assignment to non-neighborhood schools in order to achieve a given racial balance, is a political non-starter. But there is another set of alternatives that avoids the politically unacceptable choice of compulsory busing on the one hand and the socially unconscionable alternative of school segregation on the other. The whole movement toward greater choice in public education represents an opportunity. If individual preferences are honored in a way that serves larger societal interests, the advent of choice would prove a boon for integration, because it would provide an opportunity to disentangle residential segregation and school assignment. Public school choice can help close the gap between the policy consensus on the need to integrate and the political consensus against compulsory busing.

The first part of this report lays out why we believe school integration is the single most important step we can take to improve excellence and equity in education. The second part grapples directly with ways that the many obstacles to achieving integration might be addressed. The third part looks at what a number of individual communities are doing to promote more economically and racially integrated schools. In all, the report suggests some paths, grounded in real experience, toward restoring the integrated "common school"—envisioned by nineteenth-century educator Horace Mann as the "great equalizer"—for the twenty-first century.

The Importance of School Integration

The United States has a system of education that is working very well for some students and dismally failing others.[1] Low-income and minority twelfth-graders read at about the same level as more affluent and white eighth-graders.[2] Students in well-off suburban jurisdictions such as Naperville, Illinois, and Montgomery County, Maryland, score near the top in international math and science exams, while students in low-income, urban districts such as Chicago and Rochester, New York, test at the level of students in developing countries such as Iran.[3] Our schools, which Americans historically have looked to as an engine for social mobility, too often serve to perpetuate inequality.

Public officials, educators, and the media spend a great deal of time trying to address these disparities and promote greater equality of opportunity in education, but there is a stunning silence about what is known to be a leading cause of educational inequality: the degree to which poor and middle-class American schoolchildren are taught in separate settings.

We believe that school integration is imperative to promote equal educational opportunity and to forge social cohesion; to promote individual achievement and to improve life chances; and to promote the community's collective need for unity and tolerance.

Equality of Opportunity

Of all the various strategies available, research suggests that the best method for improving education in the United States is to eliminate the harmful effects of concentrated school poverty. Despite years of trying, educators have found it extremely difficult to make schools serving large numbers of low-income children provide high-quality education. While such schools exist—the Heritage Foundation found twenty-one nationally—there are some 8,600 high-poverty schools that the U.S. Department of Education calls underperforming.[4] There are no high-poverty school districts that perform at high levels.[5] All students—middle class and poor—perform worse in high-poverty schools. One Department of Education study found that low-income children attending middle-class schools perform better, on average, than middle-class children attending high-poverty schools.[6]

By the same token, all children—middle class, poor, black, white, Asian, and Latino—achieve better in integrated, middle-class schools than they do in poverty-concentrated schools. Dozens of studies, dating back to the seminal 1966 Coleman Report, find that low-income children have higher levels of achievement, and/or larger achievement gains over time, when they attend middle-class schools than when they attend high-poverty schools.[7] A 1999 Department of Education study, for example, found that "poor students in high-poverty schools are doubly at risk, with lower achievement levels than poor students in low-poverty schools."[8] The notion that all children perform better in middle-class schools than in poverty-concentrated schools, says Harvard's Gary Orfield, "is one of the most consistent findings in research on education."[9] Indeed, one reason that intergenerational white poverty is less prevalent than intergenerational black poverty is that poor, white children are much more likely than poor, African-American children to live in middle-class neighborhoods and attend good schools.[10] Middle-class schools work, and that success has been replicated thousands of times over.

How important is school socioeconomic status to individual achievement? Some studies find it is as important as the income of the student's family and home environment.[11] Likewise, Robert Crain of Columbia has found that racial desegregation, when begun early, can result in a black achievement gain of roughly one grade level. His 1996 study of black test scores in thirty-two states found that the achievement gap on fourth-grade reading was largest in states such as New York and Michigan, where African Americans were most isolated, and smallest in Iowa and West Virginia, where blacks are more integrated.[12]

Low-income and minority children also have higher graduation and college attendance rates and better job prospects when they attend middle-class, integrated schools. For example, a 2001 study by University of Chicago researcher Jonathan Guryan found that school desegregation accounted for roughly half the decline in black dropout rates between 1970 and 1980, and had no effect on the dropout rate of whites.[13] In 1996, University of California–Berkeley researcher Claude Fischer found that, controlling for individual ability and family home environment, attending a middle-class school reduced the chances of adult poverty by more than two-thirds (4 percent versus 14 percent).[14]

Why do children from all backgrounds do better in majority middle-class schools? Why does it matter whom you sit next to in class? A number of studies find that schools with a core of middle-class families are marked by higher expectations, higher-quality teachers, more-motivated students, more financial resources, and greater parental involvement. In short, virtually all of the essential features that educators identify as markers of good schools are much more likely to be found in middle-class than in high-poverty schools.

Middle-class parents are more likely to have the political savvy and pull to demand adequate financial resources from public coffers than low-income parents and often supplement these funds with private donations.[15] Middle-class parents are in a position to be more active in schools (they are four times as likely to be members of the PTA than low-income parents) and insist on high standards.[16] One national study found that the grade of A in a low-income school is the equivalent of the grade of C in a middle-class school.[17]

While students of all economic backgrounds add value to our schools, more-affluent classmates bring from home more academic knowledge, on average, which they share informally with classmates every day. For example, middle-class children come to school with a vocabulary that is four times the size of low-income children, on average; so low-income children attending middle-class schools are exposed to and benefit from a much richer vocabulary in the classroom and on the playground.[18] Likewise, middle-class children are about half as likely to engage in disruptive behavior in school as low-income children, in large measure because the life experience of middle-class students is more supportive of the notion that educational achievement will pay off.[19]

Moreover, as a consequence of the related environment and working conditions, high-quality teachers gravitate toward middle-class schools. Teachers in middle-class schools are more likely to teach in their field of expertise; more likely to have higher teacher test scores; and more likely to be experienced.[20] A great deal of new evidence confirms that teacher quality has a profound effect on student achievement.[21]

Conversely, the pervasive effects of inequality that stem from concentrated poverty help explain why traditional efforts that attempt to address inequality piece by piece often fail to make significant inroads. Much effort is placed, for example, in providing financial equity for low-income schools—a program that we support—but despite the expenditure of large amounts of compensatory spending in this nation and others, the results are mixed. Even in communities where high-poverty districts outspend more affluent districts, performance has been disappointing.[22] Likewise, efforts to recruit high-quality teachers to economically segregated schools through bonuses often have been unsuccessful because they do not address the underlying working conditions that make teaching in such schools so difficult.[23] Teacher-seniority rules, which give experienced teachers priority in deciding which schools they will teach in, further complicate equity in teaching. It may well be that the *only* way that large numbers of low-income students will have access to consistent high-quality teachers is in integrated schools.

Segregation has a way of undercutting even good programs. For instance, class-size reduction is a smart policy, but in a segregated setting, the resulting increased demand for teachers has led middle-class schools to hire away the best teachers from low-income schools.[24] So, too, spending equalization is a sound policy, but in a segregated context, wealthy parents will supplement school spending with private donations, creating a new form of inequality.[25] Indeed, given the powerful influence of parents and peers, by definition, we cannot provide full educational opportunity in a segregated environment.

None of this discussion should be taken as a condemnation of individual low-income students, parents, or communities. For example, to observe that low-income parents, on average, are less likely to volunteer in the classroom reflects in some large measure the fact that low-income employees are less likely to have the flexibility to take time off work, and that low-income parents may be intimidated by educators who sometimes mistreat them. But segregation, for a variety of reasons, undercuts opportunity, and it must be addressed if this nation is to be serious about providing equal educational opportunity.

Social Cohesion

Integration is not just about test scores; it is about building character, promoting tolerance, and reducing social ignorance. We are reminded, in the wake of the September 11 terrorist attacks, of the critical role that American public schools can play in forging unity amidst diversity and teaching common democratic values. Americans invented "common schools"—schools educating children of all different incomes, races, and religious backgrounds under one roof—and today they must be reinvented to produce not only high-skilled workers but also active citizens, loyal Americans, and tolerant adults.

In 1948, Felix Frankfurter wrote that American public education is "the most powerful agency for promoting cohesion among heterogeneous democratic people . . . at once the symbol of our democracy and the most pervasive means for promoting our common destiny."[26] Economically and racially integrated schools also have a much better chance of reinforcing important lessons about democracy and tolerance, while segregated schools often foster distrust of the "other." An array of studies find that students who attend integrated schools are more likely to live integrated lives as adults and to be more tolerant.[27] Preventing balkanization through public schools is more important than ever, both because our nation is growing increasingly diverse and because the other major public institution that promoted economic and racial mixing—the military draft—has been eliminated.

Rising Segregation: The Need for Immediate Action

Integration will not happen by itself. While polls find Americans are more tolerant than ever, entrenched residential patterns persist, and public inattention to the issue of segregation has taken its toll. Indeed, research shows that the problem of economic and racial school segregation is getting worse, not better. As David Rusk finds in his background paper for this Task Force, American public elementary schools became more economically segregated in the 1990s, a trend that parallels the rise in economic segregation by residence between 1970 and 1990. In the largest 100 metropolitan areas, economic school segregation increased in the 1990s in 55 metropolitan statistical areas, was stable in 14, and lessened in 12 (with data unavailable in 19). The nation's student population is two-thirds middle class (not eligible for federal subsidized lunches), yet one-quarter of American schools have a majority of students from low-income households.[28] Rusk also finds that while residential integration by race improved slightly during the 1990s, the segregation of black and white school children grew. He finds that declining residential segregation by race is disproportionately an adult phenomenon (integration by empty nesters and young, childless couples).

Rusk's alarming findings on the increasing economic and racial stratification of American schools dovetail with reports of the Harvard Civil Rights Project finding that more than 70 percent of American blacks now attend mostly minority schools, up from 63 percent in the 1980–81 school year.[29] The Civil Rights Project also finds that Latinos, now the largest minority group in the United States, are even more segregated in schools than are African Americans, with 76 percent of Latinos attending mostly minority schools.[30] Given the projected growth in the minority student population, and the degree to which racial segregation reinforces economic segregation, Rusk projects that economic school segregation will increase in all but six states by 2025. We are becoming two Americas—one rich, one poor—and we will pay a steep price if we do nothing to address this crisis.

The increase in residential segregation, which in turn drives school segregation, is compounded by two other factors. First is the decline in court-ordered busing. In a series of decisions in the early to mid-1990s, the U.S. Supreme Court cleared the way for districts across the country to end court supervision of desegregation efforts.[31] With no new Court orders in the offing, *Brown v. Board of Education* appears to have run its course. Second, it is possible that the accountability movement is unintentionally accelerating segregation. Parents look at test scores when deciding which school districts to live in, and since test scores reflect in some large measure the socioeconomic status of families, as opposed to the value that schools are adding, people with options may increasingly gravitate toward the most affluent districts.[32]

Nearly twenty years ago, *A Nation at Risk* warned of a "rising tide of mediocrity." Policymakers responded with a number of initiatives, and today most of our nation's schools are on good footing. But many are not, and almost invariably those schools that are identified as failing are ones struggling against the effects of segregation. We feel compelled to sound the alarm over the worsening economic and racial school segregation that members of both political parties have permitted. Rather than recognize the problems segregation causes, opponents of public education have capitalized on its failures to argue for a system of private school vouchers, which only will undermine further the power of schools to provide equal opportunity and social cohesion. The situation is dire. This is hardly the time for "all deliberate speed." We never will compete fully on the international stage educationally unless we address the problem of segregation that is particularly prevalent in the United States.[33]

We recommend that federal, state, and local governments adopt a policy goal of giving every child in America the opportunity to attend an economically and racially integrated school. Every education policy decision, from the funding of multibillion-dollar federal programs to deciding where to draw a school boundary line, should weigh seriously whether the action will promote or hinder the central goal of integrated schools.

Logistical Challenges: Residential Segregation

Segregation of schools reflects segregation of neighborhoods. The "neighborhood school," a long-cherished American icon, is now a source of tremendous inequality, as advocates of vouchers implicitly acknowledge when they decry the practice of "trapping poor kids in bad schools." We recommend two complementary policies—public school choice with fairness guidelines and housing integration.

Public School Choice. Public school choice—allowing parents a choice among a variety of schools rather than automatically assigning their children to the closest school—offers an attractive way, if properly structured, to meet parental preferences for their children while also promoting school integration. Fundamentally, greater choice moves us beyond a system in which schools necessarily reflect residential segregation.

There is some evidence that unregulated public school choice actually increases segregation, however, because the most motivated middle-class families work the system to their advantage.[34] Public school choice should not be used to create the equivalent of a private school system for affluent families; it should be used to promote the best system for all students. Private preferences must be tempered by considerations of the public interest.

Controlled choice, first conceived by Charles Willie, Michael Alves, and others, provides the appropriate balance.[35] Parents in a community are polled to find out what sorts of school options they would like for their children (a Montessori school; a computer theme?) and speciality schools are created to reflect those interests. Then families rank preferences among a number of public school options within a given geographic region. The choices take place in kindergarten, the beginning of middle school, and the beginning of high school, and are decided by lottery (no camping out to be first in line). The idea is to draw zones large enough to be diverse but small enough to avoid transportation difficulties. School district officials (not individual school principals) honor choices in a way that also promotes integration, by race and/or economic class. Free transportation is provided to all students. Preferences are given to siblings of current students and students who would be able to walk to school.

Unlike magnet schools, which normally are limited in number, controlled choice has the advantage of "magnetizing" all schools in a district and avoids the creation of a two-tiered system of special magnet schools versus regular schools. Unlike open enrollment, controlled choice ensures that choice will promote, rather than undercut, student integration.

Over time, popular schools that are over-chosen can have their programs "franchised" to under-chosen schools. Under most controlled choice plans currently in operation, 90 percent of families receive one of their first three choices.[36] In large districts, choice can take place within manageable subdistricts or zones. Plans can be phased in slowly to reduce disruption.

A variant of this idea is to "magnetize" low-income students themselves. Seattle schools use a weighted funding formula, which provides extra resources to low-income students, money that travels with the students in a system of public school choice. If properly designed, such a system might promote economic integration by encouraging wealthier schools to recruit low-income students. Experience suggests, however, that the funding premium for low-income children must be very high to be effective.[37]

Public school choice necessarily means higher transportation costs for students, but they are worth paying. Over the years, opponents of integration have made great political hay over the fact that integration requires money to be spent on transportation rather than in the classroom. In fact, only a fraction of 1 percent of the nation's education budget has gone toward transportation for desegregation—although during the height of the busing controversy, polls found most Americans believed the figure to be at least 25 percent of the budget.[38] The average cost to bus the 57 percent of public school students now transported at public expense is under $500 per student.[39] Increasingly, schools are built near busy intersections, so nearby students are provided transportation for reasons of safety rather than distance. Even among children who live within one mile of their school, fewer than three in ten walk.[40] Plans to promote integration often will involve longer bus rides than current busing, but the most important point to keep in mind is that under a system of public school choice, some parents will be willing to make that tradeoff because the program at the end of the bus ride is compelling to them, while others will choose the school that is geographically closest.

Choice/Incentives. Building choice into integration plans is necessary not only to overcome the logistical obstacles associated with residential segregation, but also to provide an important political attraction for the public. Today, we have an informal system of school choice, but it is limited largely to the wealthy. Providing greater public school choice would be popular and create a way to move beyond assignment that reflects residential segregation. By 75 percent to 21 percent, Americans favor public school choice across district lines.[41] School boards also like public school choice because it avoids fights over redistricting when schools become overcrowded.

While busing for racial balance historically has been a tough political sell, it may be possible to combine growing support for the goal of integration and expanded public school choice. According to a 1998 Public Agenda survey, 76 percent of white parents opposed busing for racial balance, but 61 percent of white parents and 65 percent of black parents supported "letting parents choose their top 3 schools, where the district makes the final choice, with an eye to racial balance."[42]

Choice programs are likely to be especially effective if they rely on innovative programs to encourage integration. The central features of magnet schools are special pedagogical approaches (Montessori schools, back to basics schools, progressive education, multiple intelligence schools) or special curricular themes (computers, performing arts, international, business, science). The idea is to create schools that would not appeal to most families, but would be very appealing to some, and to draw students from a much more diverse group of families than a neighborhood school serves. Today, more students attend such public schools of choice than attend private schools.[43] Other examples of innovative programs include:

- *Extended day schools for commuting workers*. Albuquerque has implemented a successful program to draw suburban families to urban schools by providing extended day schooling, which is appealing to commuters. Parents like sharing a ride to work with their children, having them located nearby, and having extended care until the end of the workday. By reserving one-half of the school for urban students and one-half for commuters, a nice economic mix has been achieved. [44]

- *Smaller schools or class size*. Some parents may be attracted to a smaller school, or one that has smaller class size, even if the school is located farther away. Middle-class children are attending schools in New York City's District 4 and District 2 because they were offered small class sizes as an incentive.[45]

- *High-quality child care in city*. In Chicago, school officials are offering high-quality child care at elementary schools as a way of drawing middle-class families in and teaching them about what the elementary school has to offer down the line.[46]

- *Special schools linked to urban institutions.* Our nation's cities disproportionately house the leading cultural resources—universities, museums, zoos, sports facilities, centers for the performing arts, libraries, and so on—and public schools affiliated with these institutions can be popular draws for students with special interests. In Hartford, for example, an interdistrict magnet affiliated with the University of Hartford drew 1,400 applicants for 275 slots this year.[47] Likewise, urban high schools can provide internships with urban employers that may prove attractive.

Jurisdictional Challenges: Overcoming District Lines

Integration programs within district lines can accomplish a great deal because suburbs are much more economically and racially diverse than they used to be.[48] Nonurban schools enroll almost two-thirds of the nation's poor students.[49] Likewise, in several southern states, countywide school districts often include suburbs and cities within a single jurisdiction. Having said that, much segregation, particularly in the Northeast, occurs along school district lines (see Duncan Chaplin's background paper to this report), so it is important to create incentives for cross-district integration between suburbs and urban areas. (Small towns and rural areas already have the most integrated schools in the country.)[50] Some 300,000 students currently participate in interdistrict public school choice programs, over twenty times the number that use publicly funded vouchers (14,000).[51] To encourage interdistrict programs, we believe two particular strategies are worth pursuing: employing financial and legal levers.

Financial Levers. One of the enduring lessons from existing interdistrict school choice programs is the importance of providing financial incentives to both suburbs and cities to encourage integration. In St. Louis, city students transferring to the suburbs were double-funded so that the city schools did not lose all their state funding for each student who transferred out, and suburbs received significant financial supplements. The program began in the early 1980s as a court-supervised desegregation program, but in the 1990s, as the courts were signaling a willingness to end court-ordered busing nationally, the Missouri state legislature crafted a compromise, with the support of

Republican suburban legislators, to continue the program. The financial incentives were key. Some suburban legislators also realize that social science research suggests that suburbs and cities are increasingly interdependent and that to be economically successful in the long run, suburbs need thriving cities.[52]

More generally, we note that financial incentives played an important role in desegregating southern schools in the 1960s and 1970s. Desegregation accelerated dramatically once Congress passed federal aid to education and conditioned the aid on making progress in desegregation. Even though federal funds account for less than 10 percent of total education spending, all jurisdictions are now heavily dependent on those funds.[53]

Legal Levers. While the Task Force believes the primary vehicle for achieving greater equity and school integration must be the political process, historically the courts also have played an important role with regard to these issues, most notably in *Brown v. Board of Education.* As one Task Force member noted, "Imagine a world in which *Brown* had not been decided?"[54] Today, the most promising avenue is state court litigation seeking to require states to promote socioeconomic and/or racial integration to fulfill an affirmative obligation, found in many state constitutions, to provide equal educational opportunity.[55] All state constitutions make some mention of education, and to date courts in twenty states have recognized a right to an "equal" or "adequate" education.

Most of these state cases have focused on the adequacy or equity of educational spending, but in a groundbreaking 1996 decision, *Sheff v. O'Neill*, the Connecticut Supreme Court held that an equal education requires integration. The court noted that money alone was insufficient and that its earlier decision equalizing spending in *Horton v. Meskill* had not provided genuinely equal educational opportunity. Whereas *Brown v. Board of Education* reached only *de jure* segregation, *Sheff* held that *de facto* segregation is also unconstitutional as a matter of state law and established a right to integrated education that transcends district lines. Jurisdictional divides between cities and suburbs could not be used as an excuse for segregation. The decision has national implications, and efforts have already been made to replicate *Sheff* in Minneapolis, Minnesota, and Rochester, New York.[56] This type of litigation can give legislatures the political cover to do what is right and constitutionally required.

The lawyers in *Sheff* have found that establishing the legal principle is only the first step; further litigation may be required to ensure court orders actually are carried out. We urge private foundations to provide financial support for both stages in the important legal effort to promote socioeconomic and racial integration through state constitutions.

Case Studies in Integration

Cambridge, Massachusetts

Cambridge, Massachusetts, a diverse city of 100,000 that includes Harvard professors and low-income minority and white communities, was one of the first districts nationally to adopt a controlled choice system of student assignment. Originally designed to balance the student population by race, the school committee recently voted to integrate students primarily by family income.

In 1981, school officials, seeking to avoid the disturbances over busing seen in nearby Boston, sought to promote school integration through public school choice. Neighborhood schools were abolished, and now every student has the opportunity to apply to any of the fifteen K–8 schools in the district. (Cambridge has just one high school.) Under the plan, devised by Charles Willie, Michael Alves, and others, parents rank their choices when their children enter kindergarten and then a central administrator honors preferences with an eye to ensuring that the schools are also integrated, within plus or minus ten percentage points of the district average. Schools appeal to parents based on a pedagogical approach or special theme. The choice mechanism is also designed to provide new data each year to school officials about what schools are popular (overchosen) and unpopular (underchosen). In theory, officials then can take corrective action at unpopular schools (firing principals, reconstituting schools with a new, more attractive theme).

Over the years, the plan proved highly effective at reconciling integration and choice. All the schools have been racially diverse, and more than 90 percent of students attend one of their parents' first three choices. But in recent years, school officials began considering a significant change. Looking, again, across the river to Boston, they saw that the use of race in student assignment was vulnerable from a legal standpoint, and they found that integrating by race did not by itself prevent poverty isolation and its academic effects. While each school was racially balanced, some schools were predominantly middle class and others were predominantly poor, with the portion of students eligible for free and reduced-price lunch ranging from 20 percent to 80 percent. The other limitation was one of implementation: over the years, superintendents had not taken the hard steps of reconstituting underchosen schools; choice was not an automatically self-correcting process in which unpopular schools were upgraded.

In December 2001, the Cambridge School Committee, relying on local school data and national studies finding that all students do better in middle-class schools, voted six to zero to adopt a plan to balance the schools by socioeconomic status. In the first year, 2002–03, the goal is for each school to be within fifteen percentage points, plus or minus, the district average for free and reduced-price lunch eligibility (currently 48 percent). In subsequent years, the permissible range will be reduced to 10 percent, then 5 percent. The board also put in place a mechanism to ensure continued racial diversity. School officials believe they are taking an innovative student-assignment program that has achieved racial diversity through choice and turning it into an even better program to raise student achievement.

St. Louis, Missouri

St. Louis, Missouri, has the largest interdistrict integration program in the nation with as many as 13,000 urban students attending suburban schools and another 1,500 suburban students attending urban schools. Initially part of a 1980s court-approved racial desegregation settlement, the plan was, in the late 1990s, voluntarily extended by state legislators to the surprise of many.

In the early 1970s, plaintiffs sued to overturn *de jure* segregation in St. Louis and the surrounding suburbs. In most jurisdictions around the country, suburban communities were not included in urban desegregation plans because they were not guilty of segregation; but St. Louis proved an exception to this rule because there was evidence that the suburbs and state were culpable parties. A federal judge threatened to consolidate St. Louis and suburban schools into a single district, but the state and suburban jurisdictions settled the suit, with an agreement to allow black students to transfer to suburban schools until between 15 percent and 25 percent of the student population was black. The state agreed to pay for transportation and for the entire cost of educating transfer students, and also to continue paying one-half the state aid to St. Louis schools for each student who left. Under the plan, black city students could choose to transfer to any of 122 schools in sixteen suburban districts. The scheme also provided funding for urban magnet schools to attract white suburban students.

The plan generally has been considered a success: urban students who attended suburban schools were exposed to strong teaching, college fairs, and an environment of high expectations; they did better academically at the high school level and had higher graduation rates and college attendance rates than students who remained behind in city schools that received compensatory spending. Some of the success may be attributed to creaming, but not all of it, as transfer students had lower entering test scores than urban students attending city magnets, yet performed better in the end.

When the state sought to end the program in the 1990s, it met resistance not only from the NAACP but also from business leaders and suburban legislators. Business cited research that the payoff was greater for the interdistrict transfer program than investing in traditional compensatory spending schemes in urban schools. And many state legislators from suburban areas supported continuation of the program because suburban schools had become financially dependent on the resources brought by transfer students. Adjustments were made in the program; most notably, parents now choose from a limited number of suburban options within a particular zone to reduce transportation costs. As of 2002, suburbs may opt out of the program, but so far, they appear interested in participating. Elements of the program are slated to continue until 2021.

Conclusion

We recognize that promoting economically and racially integrated schools will not be easy, but just as voucher supporters doggedly try to change American education, district by district, those of us who support promoting equity in public education should engage the issue step by step. Voucher proponents have made their plan to use public funds for private schools the nation's most widely discussed education initiative despite the fact that only 14,000 students currently participate in such programs.

We believe it is possible for a small number of districts that are committed to integrated schools to lead the way. Building on one another's successes and learning from mistakes, they can begin to create a new movement to make good, once and for all, on the radical promise of American public education. We need leadership that is inspired, courageous, and determined. The obstacles are formidable, but the stakes are too high not to take action in the best interests of our children.

PUBLIC SUPPORT FOR PUBLIC SCHOOL CHOICE

RICHARD D. KAHLENBERG

Now that the Supreme Court has announced that it will decide the constitutionality of Cleveland's school voucher program, we may see an uptick in those annoyingly effective school voucher ads featuring a sympathetic African-American child, such as Ebony Johnson, who was stuck in a failing public school until a voucher program liberated her. The ads are like a continual rerun of the 2000 Republican National Convention, racially inclusive, compassionate, and conservative.

Perhaps we should be thankful that the right has, at least for the moment, shifted its strategy of putting a black face on crime and welfare, and instead is depicting African Americans as striving for educational opportunity. Still, the approach is galling to those of us who don't see privatizing education as the next civil rights movement. In any event, expect to see a lot more of this. The voucher movement has exchanged Milton Friedman for Floyd Flake. It's very smart politics, according to Terry Moe's new book, *Schools, Vouchers, and the American Public* (which, incidentally, features two African-American girls on the cover). Moe, a Stanford professor and Hoover Institution senior fellow, is an ardent voucher proponent who made his name when he published, with John Chubb, *Politics, Markets and America's Schools* in 1990. The book, which concluded that democratic control of schools is inherently inefficient and promotes bureaucracy, became the academic bible of the voucher movement.

Moe's new book is not an argument for or against vouchers; it is an analysis of public opinion on vouchers that is likely to be very influential in shaping the movement's future. Moe has written a nuanced and

---

Originally published as "The Voucher Wars," a review of Terry M. Moe, *Schools, Vouchers, and the American Public* (Washington, D.C.: Brookings Institution Press, 2001), in *The Nation*, November 26, 2001, © 2001. Reprinted with permission.

thoughtful treatise that goes beneath the notoriously unreliable single-shot question favored by the media: Do you favor or oppose school vouchers?

The simple yes-or-no question is unhelpful, Moe notes, in part because most Americans don't know what to think. "Despite all the political turmoil at the elite level," Moe writes, "fully 65% of Americans say they have not heard about vouchers." To the extent people know what they're talking about, they are torn, Moe finds—all of which means the future of school vouchers is very much up for grabs.

Moe found in his 1995 nationally representative survey of 4,700 adults that voucher proponents have a couple of things going for them, and some substantial obstacles as well. Champions of vouchers will be pleased to know that, fundamentally, most Americans think the current system of public education is highly inequitable and needs reform. Sixty-four percent of Americans agree that "families with low incomes often have little choice but to send their children to schools that are not very good." Moe returns to this theme throughout the book and concludes that "the equity issue is central to the way Americans think about their education system, and is potentially a very powerful appeal of the voucher movement as it seeks to attract support." Moe predicts that the equity theme will ultimately lead civil rights groups, which now oppose vouchers, to switch sides, leaving teachers' unions alone in defense of the status quo. (The one caveat Moe introduces is that low-income and less-educated parents are more satisfied with their schools, even though, objectively, they have the most reason to complain.)

The other good news for voucher proponents, Moe finds, is that most Americans think private schools do a better job of educating students than public schools. Fifty-seven percent of Americans think private and parochial schools rank better, not worse, in academic quality (5 percent rank them worse, 27 percent rank them about the same and 11 percent don't know). In predicting the future of vouchers, Moe writes, "it is of enormous importance that most people think private schools are superior to public schools." Along the same lines, people like the idea of having more choice among schools, both because they want the opportunity to better match schools to their children's individual needs and because the discipline of competition may yield school improvement.

On the other hand, Moe finds that voucher opponents have two key sources of public support. Most important, Moe says, is that Americans have a "public school ideology." He explains: "Many Americans simply like the idea of a public school system. They see it as an expression of local democracy and a pillar of the local community, [and] they admire the egalitarian principles on which it is based." The corollary of this finding is that Americans are risk averse about privatization schemes and favor heavy regulation of private-school vouchers. Under plans where public dollars are to be used for private school tuition, Moe finds that 88 percent favor private-school-teacher certification requirements, 80 percent favor curriculum requirements, 83 percent financial reporting and auditing requirements, and 86 percent student testing. Americans also favor strong equity provisions: Eighty-two percent say parochial schools receiving vouchers should have to admit students of all religions, and 75 percent support a set-aside or quota for low-income students. (Even 57 percent of Republicans support the set-aside.)

Moe suggests that all this means that voucher advocates—at least initially—should focus on targeted, means-tested and highly regulated voucher programs, and that purist voucher supporters should learn to live with these conditions in order to blunt public concerns about vouchers. This line of thinking is similar to that advanced over the years by liberals like Robert Reich and Christopher Jencks, and by John Coons and Stephen Sugarman in their book *Education by Choice*. Moe does not fully address the problems of supply these regulations might create. There is evidence, in Florida and Milwaukee, that the more regulations placed on schools to qualify for vouchers, the fewer the number of schools that will participate. Some 70 percent of Catholic high schools require a test for admission, and it is not at all clear how many private schools would be willing to admit students by lottery, much less set aside slots for low-income children. Nor is it clear how many schools would go along with strict accountability provisions. Significantly, President Bush's federal voucher proposal did not call for testing in private schools, though tests are at the center of his efforts to improve public schools.

What do all the book's data mean for progressives? Can the premise of those voucher ads—that it is unfair to trap poor and minority children in bad schools—be harnessed for progressive ends? Moe's finding that equity has a very powerful appeal, is, of course, pleasing to the liberal heart. Conservatives who, during the racial desegregation era, defended neighborhood schools as the ultimate value have now conceded that compulsory assignment of students based on what neighborhood their parents can afford to live in is unfair—and most Americans appear to agree.

Taken together with Moe's data, which find that Americans have a "normative attachment to the public schools" and want schools to be highly regulated, one obvious conclusion is that Americans will back efforts to promote greater equity and choice within the public school system. Moe himself points out that public school choice is more popular than private school choice: Seventy-five percent say parents should be able to send their children to public schools outside their district, compared with 60 percent who favor private school vouchers. In the 2000 elections, voucher initiatives in Michigan and California were overwhelmingly rejected, and this year Congress and the president quickly agreed to a compromise on vouchers that provides children in failing public schools with an option to use federal funds for transportation to better-performing public schools. At the same time, public school choice provides a more satisfying answer to families whose children are stuck in bad schools than the traditional liberal call for gradual urban school reform.

On one level, the publication of Terry Moe's book symbolizes a certain convergence in the middle. Some conservatives are now embracing highly regulated vouchers that make private schools more like public schools, while some liberals are embracing a form of public school choice that, using the competitive pressures of the market, makes public schools a little more like private schools. Under public school choice, for example, public schools need a clearly defined mission in order to attract and recruit students.

On another level, however, the difference between these two approaches remains profound. While conservatives may embrace equity and regulation in the near term, their long-term game plan looks different. Moe says that if voucher leaders want to win they "need to pursue programs targeted at disadvantaged children (at least in the short run)." Once voucher programs gain a foothold and appear less risky to the public, stage two is to universalize them. Says Moe: "The traditionalists have an advantage they can trade upon as the game is actually played out over time: most Americans believe that vouchers (if adopted) should eventually be made available to virtually all children." Already, in Milwaukee, Mayor John Norquist has proposed lifting the income caps on eligibility for the city's school voucher program, from $23,328 for a family of three to $100,000, and then eliminating the cap entirely.

This is the ultimate danger of the voucher movement. Voucher opponents are right to worry that vouchers will "drain . . . resources from the public sector." But the biggest resource isn't financial (some vouchers are so small that the per capita expenditure of remaining public school students actually increases under the plans). The far more significant drain is that of motivated families, students, and parents who have high aspirations and expectations, and put pressure on public schools to improve. At the end of the day, it is the people in a school—the students, the parents, and the teachers—who drive school quality, and when the most motivated families leave public schools, those left behind are far worse off. Such is the lesson of voucher experiments in Sweden, Chile, and New Zealand.

Public school choice, on the other hand, builds on a foundation of schools that are designed to take all comers. If greater choice is structured carefully to reduce the link between residential concentrations of poverty and school concentrations of poverty, it will have chipped away at the fountainhead of school inequality in the United States: the separate educations provided to poor and middle-class children. Moe sees public school choice as a first step toward vouchers: "Were public school choice to spread," he writes, "Americans would come to think of choice as a familiar, normal, and even necessary part of their education system—and this would encourage them to see vouchers as a closely related form of choice that is just a short step away, and not threatening or fraught with risk." But a more persuasive reading of Moe's data is that vouchers would become less viable, as Americans would see that they could get the benefits of choice (more equity and more freedom) without the dangers inherent in privatization. Americans favor the public school system for lots of good reasons—they don't like the selectivity and elitism of private education or the division inherent in private market segmentation.

Liberals can respond to the voucher movement by denouncing the exploitation of Ebony and her family for conservative ends. But the data in Terry Moe's book suggest a more constructive response. Whether intended or not, the book's polling results provide strong evidence to support a liberal counterattack that uses public school choice to help not just Ebony Johnson but her neighbors as well.

Notes

1. Introduction

The Three Liberal Responses to Private School Vouchers

1. See, for example, R. H. Melton, "Gilmore Joins GOP School Effort," *Washington Post*, September 19, 1998, p. C5 (noting five Republican governors issued a statement saying "we believe every child, regardless of social or economic status, should have the same variety of educational opportunities, wonderful teachers, and safe schools as the most privileged students enjoy").

2. See "Campaign for America's Children" (paid advertisement), *New York Times*, October 15, 2000, p. 27 (signed by Joseph Califano and Andrew Young, among others); Robert B. Reich, "The Case for 'Progressive' Vouchers," *Wall Street Journal*, September 6, 2000, p. A26; Matthew Miller, "Education: A Bold Experiment to Fix City Schools: School Vouchers," *Atlantic Monthly*, July 1999, pp. 15ff; Arthur Levine, "Why I'm Reluctantly Backing Vouchers," *Wall Street Journal*, June 15, 1998, p. A28; William Raspberry, "Jeb Bush's 'E' for Effort," *Washington Post*, March 17, 2000, p. A27; Martha Minow, "Vouching for Equality: Religious Schools Can Rank among the Choices," *Washington Post*, February 24, 2002, p. B5; "A Voucher Test," *Washington Post*, June 4, 2001, p. A18.

3. See, for example, a National Opinion Poll of the Joint Center for Political and Economic Studies, finding that in 1998, blacks ages twenty-six to thirty-five support vouchers by 64.6 to 29.3 percent. Available online at www.jointcenter.org/databank/NOP/NOP_98/Education/VOUCHERS.htm.

4. Bob Chase, president of the NEA, quoted in Richard A. Oppel, Jr., and Diana Jean Schemo, "Bush Is Warned Vouchers Might Hurt School Plans," *New York Times*, December 22, 2000, p. A1. See also Reg Weaver, "Why Schools Succeed" (paid advertisement), *Washington Post*, November 17, 2002, p. B4. In this, the new NEA president is endorsing neighborhood schools.

5. Albert Shanker, quoted in Sara Mosle, "What Really Matters in Education," *New York Times Magazine*, October 27, 1996, p. 56.

6. The St. Louis interdistrict program began as a court-supervised desegregation settlement, but in the late 1990s it survived on a voluntary basis because the business community saw the substantial educational benefits of the program and because suburban jurisdictions had grown accustomed to the

financial aid they received from the state for educating urban students. See William Freivogel, "St. Louis: Desegregation and School Choice in the Land of Dred Scott," in *Divided We Fail: Coming Together through Public School Choice: The Report of The Century Foundation Task Force on the Common School* (New York: Century Foundation Press, 2002), pp. 209–35.

2. Overview

Overblown Claims and Nagging Questions

1. "Choosing a School for Chelsea," *New York Times*, January 7, 1993, p. A22.
2. Thomas L. Friedman, "Clintons Pick Private School in Capital for Their Daughter," *New York Times*, January 6, 1993, p. A14 (emphasis added).
3. U.S. Department of Education, *Digest of Education Statistics, 1997* (Washington, D.C.: U.S. Government Printing Office, 1998), Table 120, p. 125.
4. Author's compilations from *Peterson's Private Secondary Schools, 1998–1999* (Princeton, N.J.: Peterson Publishing, 1998).
5. Milton Friedman, *Freedom and Capitalism* (Chicago: University of Chicago Press, 1962), p. 87 (emphasis added).
6. Ibid., p. 89.
7. Ibid., p. 95.
8. John E. Chubb and Terry M. Moe, *Politics, Markets, and America's Schools* (Washington, D.C.: Brookings Institution, 1990), p. 227.
9. Ibid., p. 217.
10. James S. Coleman et al., *Equality of Educational Opportunity* (Washington, D.C.: U.S. Government Printing Office, 1966).
11. George A. Clowes, "Five Steps to Full School Choice," *School Reform News* [The Heartland Institute Newsletter] (September 1998): 11 (emphasis added).
12. "Study: KC Dollar Deluge Fails to Raise Test Scores," *School Reform News* (October 1998): 1.
13. Adam Meyerson, "Education's Evil Empire," *Policy Review* (January–February 1998): 4.
14. Lowell C. Rose and Alec M. Gallup, "The 30th Annual Phi Delta Kappa/Gallup Poll of the Public's Attitudes toward the Public Schools," *Phi Delta Kappan* (September 1998): 41–56.
15. Daniel McGroarty, *Break These Chains: The Battle for School Choice* (Rocklin, Calif.: Prima, 1996), p. 74.
16. "Defaulting the Future," *U.S. News and World Report*, June 21, 1993, p. 81.
17. Rita Koselka and Suzanne Oliver, "Hairdressers, Anyone?" *Forbes*, May 22, 1995, pp. 127–28.
18. U.S. General Accounting Office, "Defaulted Student Loans: Preliminary

Analysis of Student Loan Borrowers and Defaulters," GAO/HRD-88-112BR, June 14, 1988, p. 4.

19. "Live with TAE: Milton and Rose Friedman," *American Enterprise* (January/February 1999): 20.

20. *Parental Choice Advocate: The Newsletter of the Milton and Rose D. Friedman Foundation*, July 1998, p. 6.

21. Steve Stecklow, "Florida Pact to End for Education Alternatives, Inc.," *Wall Street Journal*, May 2, 1995, p. B10.

22. "Education Alternatives, Inc. Loses Baltimore Contract," *Wall Street Journal*, December 4, 1995, p. B10.

23. Ross Kerber, "EAI Likely to Lose a Major Contract in Connecticut," *Wall Street Journal*, January 24, 1996, p. A5.

24. Cited in Ronald G. Corwin and Marcella R. Dianda, "What Can We Really Expect from Large-Scale Voucher Programs?" *Phi Delta Kappan* (September 1993): 69.

25. Ibid., 70.

26. Ibid.

27. Ibid., 69.

28. Ibid., 71.

29. Lana Muraskin and Stephanie Stullich, "Barriers, Benefits, and Costs of Using Private Schools to Alleviate Overcrowding in Public Schools," (Washington, D.C.: U.S. Department of Education, 1998), p. 61.

30. Ibid., exhibit 45, p. 69 (emphasis in original).

31. Ibid., p. 69 (emphasis in original).

32. Ibid.

33. Ibid., p. 56.

34. "The Truth . . . About Opportunity Scholarships," http://www.fcn.state.fl.us/eog/aplusplan/at_plan.

3. Myth #1: Vouchers Raise Student Achievement

The Early Reserach on School Vouchers

1. Daniel D. Goldhaber, "Public and Private High Schools: Is School Choice an Answer to the Productivity Problem?" *Economics of Education Review* 15, no. 2 (1996), p. 99 (emphasis in original).

2. Daniel D. Goldhaber, "School Choice as Education Reform," *Phi Delta Kappan* (October 1997): 145.

3. Ibid., 146 (emphasis in original).

4. James S. Coleman, T. Hoffer, and S. Kolgore, *High School Achievement: Public, Catholic, and Private Schools Compared* (New York: Basic Books, 1982).

5. Henry M. Levin, "Educational Vouchers: Effectiveness, Choice, and Costs," *Journal of Policy Analysis and Management* (September 1998): 375.

6. Derek Neal, "What Have We Learned about the Benefits of Private Schooling," *FRBNY Economic Policy Review* (March 1998): 80.

7. Anthony S. Bryk, Valerie E. Lee, and Peter B. Holland, *Catholic Schools and the Common Good* (Cambridge, Mass.: Harvard University Press, 1993). See pp. 245–71 for analysis of the academic and discipline foci; pp. 272–94 make the communal argument.

8. All enrollment figures are from the Wisconsin Department of Public Instruction's web page, http://www.dpi.state.wi.us/dpi/dfm/sms/choice

9. "1.25 Million Low-income Children Apply for 40,000 Scholarships to Attend K–8 School of Choice," Children's Scholarship Fund press release, April 21, 1999, http://www.scholarshipfund.org.

10. Connie Langland, "1,500 in Phila. Win Scholarships for Private School," *Philadelphia Inquirer,* April 22, 1999, http://www.philly.com.

11. John F. Witte, "Who Benefits from the Milwaukee Choice Program?" in Bruce Fuller and Richard F. Elmore, eds., *Who Chooses? Who Loses? Culture, Institutions, and the Unequal Effects of Choice* (New York: Teachers College Press, 1996), pp. 134–35.

12. Ibid. Demographic information is found on pp. 121–24.

13. See John F. Witte, Troy D. Sterr, and Christopher A. Thorn, "Fifth-Year Report Milwaukee Parental Choice Program," Department of Political Science and the Robert M. LaFollette Institute of Public Affairs, University of Wisconsin-Madison, December 1995, http://www.dpis.dacc.wisc.edu/choice/choice_rep95.html.

14. Ibid.

15. Ibid., pp. 126–31.

16. Paul E. Peterson, Jay P. Greene, and Chad Noyes, "School Choice in Milwaukee," *Public Interest* (Fall 1996): 50.

17. Ibid., 51 (emphasis added).

18. Ibid., 39.

19. Jay P. Greene and Paul E. Peterson, "Methodological Issues in Evaluation Research: The Milwaukee School Choice Plan," Paper for the Program in Education Policy and Governance, Department of Government and Kennedy School of Government, Harvard University, http://www.harvard.edu/pepg/witte2, p. 2.

20. Peterson, Greene, and Noyes, "School Choice in Milwaukee," 52.

21. Ibid., 55.

22. Ibid., 42.

23. Cecilia Elena Rouse, "Schools and Student Achievement: More Evidence from the Milwaukee Parental Choice Program," *FRBNY Economic Policy Review* (March 1998): 67.

24. Ibid., 68.

Recent Evidence on the Effectiveness of School Voucher Programs

1. "School Vouchers: Characteristics of Privately Funded Programs" GAO-02-752, U.S. General Accounting Office, September 2002.

2. Martin Carnoy and Patrick McEwan, "Do School Vouchers Lead to Greater Social Equity?" draft manuscript, Stanford University, September 2001.

3. "School Vouchers: Characteristics of Privately Funded Programs."

4. Cecilia Elena Rouse, "Private School Vouchers and Student Achievement: An Evaluation of the Milwaukee Parental Choice Program," *Quarterly Journal of Economics* 113, no. 2 (May 1998): 553–602.

5. Cecilia Elena Rouse, "School Reform in the 21st Century: A Look at the Effect of Class Size and School Vouchers on the Academic Achievement of Minority Students," Working Paper no. 440, Industrial Relations Section, Princeton University, June 2000.

6. Rouse, "School Reform in the 21st Century," reviews the evidence that Project STAR in Tennessee demonstrated the benefits of small classes.

7. "School Vouchers: Characteristics of Privately Funded Programs."

8. William G. Howell and Paul E. Peterson, in *The Education Gap: Vouchers and Urban Schools* (Washington, D.C.: Brookings Institution Press, 2002), place a good deal more confidence in these results than I do. For example, they note that in the middle year of the three with test results, voucher students in Washington, D.C., performed statistically better than public school students, although in the first and third year tested results were essentially identical. This appearance and subsequent disappearance of a result may simply be statistical noise. In any case, even statistically significant differences in test scores are small.

9. Alan Krueger and Pei Zhu, "Another Look at the New York City School Voucher Experiment," draft manuscript, November 2002. Paper first prepared for a "Conference on Randomized Experiments in the Social Sciences," Yale University, August 2002.

10. In the studies, race is defined by the race or ethnicity of the mother; black Hispanics are classified as Hispanic, not black. Results are sensitive to inclusion of the father's race or ethnicity and to reclassification of black Hispanics as black.

11. Hoxby's results all are reviewed in Caroline M. Hoxby, "School Choice and School Productivity (or Could School Choice Be a Tide that Lifts All Boats)," NBER Working Paper no. w8873, National Bureau of Economic Research, Cambridge, Mass., April 2002.

12. Julie Berry Cullen, Brian Jacob, and Steven Levitt, "The Impact of School Choice on Student Outcomes: An Analysis of the Chicago Public Schools," NBER Working Paper no. w7888, National Bureau of Economic Research, Cambridge, Mass., September 2000.

13. Cullen, Jacob, and Levitt measure success by graduation rates as well as by test scores.

14. Nor does Hoxby tabulate the results for productivity but rather for the numerator and denominator separately. She does report that the effect of school choice on productivity is statistically significant at the 10 percent level. We can look forward to further research that explores the robustness of these results.

15. Caroline Hoxby, personal communication.

16. It is possible that discussion of vouchers helped launch P–5 schools long before vouchers were introduced or that P–5 schools only became effective after competition from vouchers, but certainly Hoxby's conjecture cannot be accepted without further investigation.

The Problem of Taking Private School Voucher Programs to Scale

1. Paul Peterson, Address to the Heritage Foundation, May 23, 2002. (www.townhall.com/audio/content/lecture020323b.ram)

2. Brian P. Gill, P. Michael Timpane, Karen E. Ross, and Dominic J. Brewer, *Rhetoric Versus Reality: What We Know and What We Need to Know About Vouchers and Charter Schools* (Santa Monica, Calif.: Rand, 2001); William G. Howell and Paul E. Peterson, *The Education Gap: Vouchers and Urban Schools* (Washington, D.C.: Brookings Institution Press, 2002).

3. Gill et al., p. 74.

4. Howell and Peterson, p. 146, Table 6-1.

5. Howell and Peterson, p. 143.

6. Howell and Peterson, pp. 151–152.

7. Howell and Peterson, p. 208.

8. See Gill et al., pp. 86, 81, and 78, respectively.

9. See John Chubb and Terry Moe, *Politics, Markets and American Schools* (Washington, D.C.: Brookings Institution Press, 1990) (nonpolitical); James S. Coleman and Thomas Hoffer, *Public and Private High Schools: The Impact of Communities* (New York: Basic Books, 1987) (religion).

10. See, e.g., Patrick J. McEwan, *Comparing the Effectiveness of Public and Private Schools* (New York: National Center for the Study of Privatization of Education, Teachers College, Columbia, 2000); Henry M. Levin, "Educational Vouchers: Effectiveness, Choice, and Costs," *Journal of Policy Analysis and Management* 17:373–392 (1998).

11. Richard D. Kahlenberg, *All Together Now: Creating Middle Class Schools through Public School Choice* (Washington, D.C.: Brookings Institution Press, 2001), pp. 47–76.

12. Gill et al., p. xix. See also Id., p. 89.

13. Gill et al., p. xviii.

14. For a summary, see Kahlenberg, pp. 47–76.

15. David Rusk, *Inside Game Outside Game* (Washington, D.C.: Brookings Institution Press, 1998), p. 72.

16. Howell and Peterson, pp. 23–26.

17. Howell and Peterson, pp. 64, 88.

18. Howell and Peterson, p. 143.

19. Gill et al., p. 165. See also Kahlenberg, pp. 98–99.

20. Howell and Peterson, pp. 62–64.

21. Howell and Peterson, p. 78, Table 3-10.

22. Howell and Peterson, p. 165, citing Caroline Hoxby, "Peer Effects in the Classroom: Learning from Gender and Race Variation," Working Paper 7867 (Cambridge, Mass: National Bureau of Economic Research, August 2000). Howell and Peterson try to downplay the issue, noting that their polls of students found "little change in student friendship patterns." Howell and Peterson, p. 165. But this response ignores the findings of many researchers that peer effects go far beyond close friends to include all sorts of classmates. See studies cited in Kahlenberg, pp. 143–144.

23. Howell and Peterson, p. 110. Howell and Peterson found that school disruption did explain student performance but not why African Americans did particularly well. Id, p. 160. However, they acknowledge this could stem from inaccurate measurements. Id, p. 164.

24. Howell and Peterson, p. 34 (money down), Howell and Peterson, p. 116 (parents active).

25. Howell and Peterson, p. 165.

26. Kahlenberg, pp. 67–72.

27. There are other problems associated with taking voucher programs to scale. To accommodate increased demand, new voucher schools that pop up in response may very well be of lower quality than existing private schools. See Gordon MacInnes, "Kids Who Pick the Wrong Parents and Other Victims of Voucher Schemes," The Century Foundation, New York, 1999, pp. 29–32.

28. This is analogous to what happened in universal voucher programs where the most motivated and wealthy families left and those remaining in public school were worse off. See discussion of studies in Chile and New Zealand in Kahlenberg, p. 97.

29. Howell and Peterson, p. 205 (citing research by Jay Greene in Florida indicating improvement in public schools from the threat of vouchers, but noting also that the results are disputed because it may have been other accountability provisions that resulted in improved performance).

30. Howell and Peterson, p. 41 (citing research by Jens Ludwig, Helen Ladd and Gregory Duncan).

31. For a discussion of these studies, see Kahlenberg, pp. 39–40.

32. Gill et al., p. 223.

33. Steve Farkas and Jean Johnson, *Time to Move On: African-American and*

White Parents Set an Agenda for Public Schools (New York: Public Agenda, 1998), p. 41.

34. Kahlenberg, pp. 104, 228–257. See also *Divided We Fail: Coming Together through Public School Choice: Report of The Century Foundation Task Force on the Common School* (New York: Century Foundation Press, 2002).

35. Terry Moe, *Schools, Vouchers and the American Public* (Washington, D.C: Brookings Institution Press, 2001), p. 333.

36. Howell and Peterson, pp. 11–12.

4. Myth #2: Vouchers Are Part of the New Civil Rights Movement

Vouchers and Segregation

1. Even Catholic schools, which are traditionally less selective than other private schools, often require admissions tests. At the high school level, 70 percent of Catholic schools require students to take an admissions test. See Anthony S. Bryk, Valerie E. Lee, and Peter B. Holland, *Catholic Schools and the Common Good* (Cambridge, Mass.: Harvard University Press, 1993), p. 128. Some 40 percent of Catholic elementary and secondary schools now have waiting lists. See Timothy Egan, "The Changing Face of Catholic Education," *New York Times Education Life*, August 6, 2000, p. 28.

2. In Florida, where the voucher statute included a requirement of lottery admission, just 7 percent of the state's private schools signed up to take part in the program even after state officials extended the deadline. Robert Sanchez, "Few Schools Joining Plan," *Miami Herald*, April 18, 2000, p. 1B, and Leslie Clark, "More Schools Willing to Use Vouchers," *Miami Herald*, May 23, 2000, p. 1A.

3. See Martin Carnoy, "National Voucher Plans in Chile and Sweden: Did Privatization Reforms Make for Better Education?" *Comparative Education Review*, August 1998, pp. 309, 318, 320, 333–36; Fiske and Ladd, *When Schools Compete*; Rusk, Frieling, and Groenemejjer, *Inside Game/Outside Game: Segregation and Spatial Planning.*

4. *Digest of Education Statistics, 2000* (Washington, D.C.: U.S. Department of Education, 2001), Table 60.

5. Albert Shanker, quoted in Sara Mosle, "What Really Matters in Education," *New York Times Magazine*, October 27, 1996, p. 56.

6. Helen Dewar, "Senate Drops Vouchers from Education Bill," *Washington Post*, June 13, 2001, p. A12.

Charter Schools and Racial and Social Class Segregation

1. Gary Orfield, "Public Opinion and School Desegregation," *Teachers College Record* 96, no. 4 (1995): 654–70.

2. *Time to Move On* (Washington, D.C.: Public Agenda, 1998).

3. Amy Stuart Wells and Robert L. Crain, "Perpetuation Theory and the Long-term Effects of School Desegregation" *Review of Educational Research* 64, no. 4 (1994): 531–55.

4. Ibid.

5. Gary Orfield et al., "Deepening Segregation in American Public Schools," Harvard Project on School Desegregation Report, Harvard University, 1997.

6. Darcia Harris Bauman, "South Carolina Charter School Law Still in Limbo," *Education Week*, July 12, 2000, p. 28.

7. Geoff Whitty, "Creating Quasi-Markets in Education: A Review of Recent Research on Parental Choice and School Autonomy in Three Countries," *Review of Research in Education*, vol. 22 (1997): 3–47.

8. See, for example, Bruno V. Manno et al., "How Charter Schools Are Different: Lessons and Implications from a National Study," *Phi Delta Kappan* 79, no. 7 (March 1998): 488–98; Louann Bierlein, "Charter Schools: A New Approach to Public Education," *NASSP Bulletin* 79, no. 572 (September 1995): 12–20.

9. See Roselyn Tantraphol, "Debater Says School Choice Is a Question of Civil Rights," *The Union-News*, March 2, 2000, http://www.massline.com; Nina Shokraii, "Free at Last: Black American Signs up for School Choice," *Policy Review* 80 (November–December 1996): 20–26; Lynn Schnaiberg, "Justice Department Accused of Obstructing Charter Schools" *Education Week*, October 20, 1999.

10. See, for example, Gregg Vanourek et al., *Charter Schools in Action: Charter Schools as Seen by Those Who Know Them Best: Students, Teachers, and Parents* (Washington, D.C.: The Hudson Institute, June 1997), http://www.edexcellence.net/chart/chart2html; *The State of Charter Schools: Third-year Report 1999*, conducted by RPP International (Washington, D.C.: U.S. Department of Education, Office of Educational Research and Improvement, May 1999), http://www.ed.gov/pubs/charter3rdyear/title.html.

11. We draw from a number of independently conducted studies of charter schools in various states. Thus, we have excluded reports by partisan think tanks that simultaneously support charter school reform. The problem with this analysis is that each of these studies was designed to answer a different set of research questions, each draws from a different body of data, and employs different

definitions and measures. For instance, in some reports the researchers did not consider a charter school's enrollment to be racially or ethnically distinct from that of the state or district enrollment unless they differed by 20 percent or more. Other researchers considered charter school to be distinct if their enrollments in one or more racial/ethnic category differed by only 10 percent. Also, depending on the way in which the data are presented in the reports, it was often impossible to reanalyze them to make the findings more uniform. Still, we have made the effort to contrast and compare the information in each report as best we can.

12. See the Center for Education Reform's website for information on their state ranking system: http://edreform.com/charter_schools/laws/ranking.htm.

Choosing Segregation

1. Dan D. Goldhaber, "Public and Private High Schools: Is School Choice an Answer to the Productivity Problem?" *Economics of Education Review* 15, no. 2 (1996): 101.

2. David Tyack and Larry Cuban, *Tinkering Toward Utopia: A Century of Public School Reform* (Cambridge, Mass.: Harvard University Press, 1995), p. 29.

3. Jeffrey R. Henig, "The Local Dynamics of Choice: Ethnic Preferences and Institutional Responses," in Bruce Fuller and Richard F. Elmore, eds., *Who Chooses? Who Loses? Culture, Institutions, and the Unequal Effects of Choice* (New York: Teachers College Press, 1996), p. 112.

4. Henig, "The Local Dynamics of Choice," p. 105.

5. Ibid., p. 114.

6. Amy Stuart Wells, "African-American Students' View of School Choice," in Fuller and Elmore, eds., *Who Chooses? Who Loses?* p. 32.

7. Ibid., p. 34.

8. Ibid., p. 35.

9. Ibid., p. 36.

10. Ibid., pp. 45–57.

11. Valerie Martinez, Kenneth Godwin, and Frank R. Kemerer, "Public School Choice in San Antonio: Who Chooses and with What Effects?" in Fuller and Elmore, eds., *Who Chooses? Who Loses?* p. 56.

12. Ibid., Table 3.2, p. 58.

5. Myth #3: Vouchers Promote Democracy

Religious Schooling with Public Dollars

1. National Center for Education Statistics, U.S. Department of Education, *Digest of Education Statistics, 1997* (Washington, D.C.: U.S. Government Printing Office, December 1997), p. 70.

2. Ibid., p. 15.

3. Ibid., and Frank H. Bredeweg, "United States Catholic Elementary and Secondary Schools, 1987–88," National Catholic Educational Association, 1988, p. 15.

4. Calculations by David P. Baker and Cornelius Riordan, "The 'Eliting' of the Common American Catholic School and the National Education Crisis," *Phi Delta Kappan* (September 1998): 16–23; income information on p. 19.

5. Scott Stephens and Mark Vosburgh, "Voucher School Relies on Videos as Teachers," *Plain Dealer*, July 10, 1999, http://www.cleveland.com/news/sreports.

6. Scott Stephens and Mark Vosburgh, "Murderer on Staff of State-funded Private School," *Plain Dealer*, July 1, 1999, http://www.cleveland.com/news/sreports.

7. National Catholic Educational Association, "United States Catholic Elementary and Secondary Schools, 1997–98," Washington, D.C., 1998, p. 13.

6. Myth #4: American Public Is Clamoring for Vouchers

Congress and School Vouchers

1. Jill Zuckman. "School 'Choice' a Tough Choice for Members of Congress," *Congressional Quarterly*, April 27, 1991, pp. 1061–2.

2. Jill Zuckman, "New Bill Kills Federal Money for Private School 'Choice,'" *Congressional Quarterly*, February 29, 1992, pp. 471–72.

3. Jill Zuckman, "School Standards Approved along Party-Line Vote," *Congressional Quarterly*, June 26, 1993, p. 1663.

4. Dana Milbank, "Bush Makes Education 1st Initiative," *Washington Post*, January 24, 2001, p. A1.

5. Dana Milbank, "Bush Likely to Drop Vouchers; Education Policy to Focus on Testing, States' Flexibility," *Washington Post*, January 2, 2001, p. A1.

6. "House Vote 524. HR 2646," *CQ Almanac 1997*, p. H-160.

7. "Private School Aide Bill Blocked by Critics," *CQ Almanac 1997*, pp. 7.6–7.7.

8. "House vote 243. HR 2646," *CQ Almanac 1998*, p. H-70.

9. "Senate vote 169. HR 2646," *CQ Almanac 1998*, p. S-28.

10. "President Blocks GOP Drive to Give Tax Breaks for Education Savings Accounts," *CQ Almanac, 1998*, pp. 9.14–9.18.

11. "Senate Panel Votes to Expand Education Savings Accounts to Include Elementary, Secondary School," *CQ Weekly*, March 17, 2002, p. 610.

8. Public School Choice: Student Achievement, Integration, Democracy, and Public Support

Equitable Public School Choice

1. See Charles V. Willie and Michael Alves, *Controlled Choice: A New Approach to Desegregated Education and School Improvement* (Providence, R.I.: Education Alliance Press and the New England Desegregation Assistance Center of Brown University, 1996); Charles L. Glenn, *Family Choice and Public Schools: A Report to the State Board of Education* (Quincy, Mass.: Massachusetts Department of Education, January 1986) ("conditional choice").

2. Michael Alves and Charles V. Willie, "Controlled Choice—An Approach to Effective School Desegregation," *Urban Review 19* (1987), p. 76.

3. Ibid., p. 81. Education Commission of the States, *A State Policy-Makers' Guide to Public-School Choice*, draft (Denver: Education Commission of the States, February 1989), p. 34. Under "preferred choice," parents choose among schools and are assigned with an eye to demographic balance but are guaranteed admission to their home district school, at the least; see Dan Beyers, "County Looks at Changes in School Choice Plan," *Washington Post*, October 3, 1996, p. Md1. Another alternative is "limited controlled choice," in which students attend neighborhood schools unless there is an imbalance, in which case new students are transferred to address the imbalance; David J. Armor, *Forced Justice: School Desegregation and the Law* (New York: Oxford University Press, 1995), p. 163. A third variation assigns students to neighborhood schools but allows them to transfer to another school in the district if there is space and the change does not contribute to racial imbalance; Timothy W. Young and Evans Clinchy, *Choice in Public Education* (New York: Teachers College Press, 1992), pp. 39–41. A fourth variation is "Equity Choice," in which students may choose any public or private school but transportation is paid only if the transfer improves the "racial (or possibly economic) balance of the sending and receiving schools"; see Armor, *Forced Justice*, pp. 228–29.

4. See Evans Clinchy, interview by author, Boston, November 21, 1997.

5. See Willie and Alves, *Controlled Choice: A New Approach to Desegregated Education and School Improvement* (1996), p. ii; Jeffrey R. Henig, *Rethinking School Choice: Limits of the Marketplace Metaphor* (Princeton University Press, 1994), p. 257 n.30; Young and Clinchy, *Choice in Public Education*, pp. 6, 32; Armor, *Forced Justice*, pp. 48, 168–69; Christine H. Rossell, "The Buffalo Controlled Choice Plan," *Urban Education*, vol. 22 (October 1987), p. 328; Charles Glenn, "Parent Choice and American Values," in Joe Nathan, ed., *Public Schools by Choice: Expanding Opportunities for Parents, Students, and Teachers* (St. Paul, Minn.: Institute for Learning and Teaching, 1989), p. 42; Peter Schmidt, "Problems with Launch of Choice Plan Place Indianapolis Official under Fire," *Education Week*, September 29, 1993, p. 8; Anne Lindberg, "Busing: Where Are We Headed?" *St. Petersburg Times*, Aug. 26, 1996, p. 1A; Brian Hicks, "Some Families Find the Choice Limited," *Charleston Post and Courier*, May 3, 1998, p. A1; Caroline Hendrie, "Without Court Orders, Schools Ponder How to Pursue Diversity," *Education Week*, April 30, 1997.

6. Charles Glenn, "Controlled Choice in Massachusetts Public Schools," *Public Interest*, vol. 103 (Spring 1991), p. 92. Henig, *Rethinking School Choice*, p. 90; William Bennett, *American Education: Making it Work* (Government Printing Office, 1998), p. 47; Norma Tan, *The Cambridge Controlled Choice Program: Improving Educational Equity and Integration* (New York: Manhattan Institute, 1990), p. 11. The controlled choice plan in Little Rock, Arkansas, was dismantled after a single year following rushed implementation; see Hicks, "Some Families Find the Choice Is Limited," p. A1. The controlled choice plan, adopted by Seattle, Washington, in 1988, was ended in 1996; see Caroline Hendrie, "Seattle to Shelve Race-Based Busing in Shift toward Neighborhood Schools," *Education Week*, December 4, 1996. The judicial shift on racial integration has resulted in the termination of controlled choice in Boston and Indianapolis; see Caroline Hendrie, "Judge Spurns Indianapolis Bid to Recover Bused Students," *Teacher Magazine*, March 12, 1997, and discussion of Boston in chapter 8.

7. National Governors' Association, *Time for Results: The Governors' 1991 Report on Education* (Washington: National Governors' Association Center for Policy Research and Analysis, 1986), p. 70. For Cambridge, see Tan, *The Cambridge Controlled Choice Program*, pp. 12–14; Jaclyn Fierman, "Giving Parents a Choice of Schools," *Fortune*, December 4, 1989, p. 150; Young and Clinchy, *Choice in Public Education*, p. 31; Henig, *Rethinking School Choice*, p. 123; Christine H. Rossell and Charles L. Glenn, "The Cambridge Controlled Choice Plan," *Urban Review*, vol. 20 (summer 1988), pp. 89–90; Amy Stuart Wells, *Time to Choose: America at the Crossroads of School Choice Policy* (New York: Hill and Wang, 1993), p. 90; Michael Alves, "Maximizing Parental Choice and Effective Desegregation Outcomes: The Cambridge Plan" in Charles Glenn, ed., *Family Choice and Public Schools: A Report to the State Board*

of Education, pp. 48, 53; Alves and Willie, "Controlled Choice—An Approach to Effective School Desegregation," pp. 85–86. For Montclair, see Beatriz C. Clewell and Myra F. Joy, *Choice in Montclair, New Jersey* (Princeton, N.J.: Educational Testing Service, 1990), pp. 5–6, 12, 31–33; Young and Clinchy, *Choice in Public Education*, p. 22; Henig, *Rethinking School Choice*, pp. 123–24; Jaclyn Fierman, "Giving Parents a Choice of Schools, *Fortune*, December 4, 1989, p. 150; William Snider, "The Call for Choice: Competition in the Educational Marketplace," *Education Week*, June 24, 1987, p. C9; Jane Manners, "Repackaging Segregation: A History of the Magnet School System in Montclair, New Jersey," *Race Traitor*, vol. 8 (winter 1998), pp. 52–55; in the late 1990s, the schools remained solidly balanced, with all elementary schools within a range between 44 percent to 56 percent white; see Montclair Public School System, *Report of District Enrollment*, pp. 11, 14. For Buffalo, see David T. Kearns and Denis P. Doyle, *Winning the Brain Race: A Bold Plan to Make Our Schools Competitive* (San Francisco, Calif.: Institute for Contemporary Studies Press, 1988), p. 29; Rossell, "The Buffalo Controlled Choice Plan," pp. 334, 344, 350–51. For Lowell, see Young and Clinchy, *Choice in Public Education*, p. 80.

8. See Lauri Steel and Roger Levine, *Educational Innovation in Multiracial Contexts* (Palo Alto, Calif.: American Institutes for Research, 1994), p. 4.

9. James S. Coleman, "Racial Segregation in the Schools: New Research with New Policy Implications," *Phi Delta Kappan*, vol. 57 (October 1975), p. 78; David J. Armor, "After Busing: Education and Choice," *Public Interest* (spring 1989), pp. 24–25. On parents' impotence under forced busing, see the discussion in chapter 8. Nathan quoted in Carol Steinbach and Neal R. Pierce, "Multiple Choice," *National Journal*, July 1, 1989, p. 1693. Education Commission of the States, *A State Policy-Makers' Guide*, p. 3. Bella Rosenberg, "Public School Choice: Can We Find the Right Balance?" *American Educator*, vol. 13 (summer 1989), p. 12. Alves, "Maximizing Parental Choice," pp. 39–40. Ronald E. Koetzch, *The Parents' Guide to Alternatives in Education* (Boston: Shambhala, 1997); Snider, "The Call for Choice," pp. C19–C20.

10. Thomas Toch, "Schools that Work," *U.S. News and World Report*, October 7, 1996, pp. 58–64. Amy Stuart Wells, "Once a Desegregation Tool, Magnet Schools become Schools of Choice," *New York Times*, January 9, 1991. See, for example, Wilson, *When Work Disappears*, p. 214; Seymore Fliegel, with James MacGuire, *Miracle in East Harlem: The Fight for Choice in Public Education* (Random House, 1993), pp. 3–4, 14; Anemona Hartocollis, "Choice System Helps Schools in East Harlem," *New York Times*, February 24, 1998, pp. B1, B5.

11. Evans Clinchy and Frances Arick Kolb, eds., *Planning for School Choice: Achieving Equity and Excellence* (Andover, Mass.: NETWORK, 1989), pp. 5–6.

12. See Caroline M. Hoxby, "What Do America's 'Traditional' Forms of School Choice Teach Us about School Choice Reforms?" *FRBNY Economic Policy Review*, vol. 4, no. 1 (March 1998), pp. 52–55; Joseph S. Tracy and

Barbara L. Walter, "Summary of Observations and Recommendations," in id., pp. 4, 6; Education Commission of the States, *A State Policy-Makers' Guide*, p. 3; Gary Putka, "Choose-a-School: Parents in Minnesota Are Getting to Send Kids Where They Like," *Wall Street Journal*, May 13, 1988, p. A1; Edward Fiske, "Wave of the Future: A Choice of Schools," *New York Times*, June 4, 1989, p. 32; Joe Nathan, "Charters and Choice," *American Prospect* (November–December 1998), p. 75; June Kronholz, "Charter Schools Begin to Prod Public Schools toward Competition," *Wall Street Journal*, February 12, 1999, p. A1; Thomas Toch, *Improving Performance: Competition in American Public Education* (Washington: National Alliance of Business, 2000), p. 10.

13. Adam Urbanski, "Make Public Schools More Like Private Schools," *Education Week*, January 31, 1996, pp. 31, 33. Kristina Torres, "Controlled Choice? Boston Gives Plan a Passing Grade," *Charleston Post and Courier*, May 3, 1998, p. A1; Glenn, "Controlled Choice in Massachusetts Public Schools," p. 95; "Quality Counts '98," p. 45.

14. See, for example, Patricia A. Bauch, *Family Choice and Parental Involvement in Inner-City Catholic High Schools: An Exploration of Psycho-Social and Organizational Factors* (Catholic University Press, 1987), p. 20. Deborah Meier, *The Power of Their Ideas: Lessons for America from a Small School in Harlem* (Boston: Beacon Press, 1995), p. 101.

15. National Governors' Association, *Time for Results*, p. 68. Bauch, *Family Choice and Parental Involvement*, p. 3. Kearns and Doyle, *Winning the Brain Race*, p. 29; David W. Kirkpatrick, *Choice in Schooling: A Case for Tuition Vouchers* (Loyola University Press, 1990), pp. 91–95; Witte, "Who Benefits from the Milwaukee Choice Program?" p. 132; Gary Orfield, *City-Suburban Desegregation: Parent and Student Perspectives in Metropolitan Boston* (Cambridge, Mass.: Harvard Civil Rights Project, September 1997), p. 22; Mark Schneider and others, "Institutional Arrangements and the Creation of Social Capital: The Effects of Public School Choice," *American Political Science Review*, vol. 91 (March 1997), pp. 82, 84–86, 88–90.

16. Young and Clinchy, *Choice in Public Education*, p. 114.

17. See *Pasadena City Board of Education v. Spangler*, 427 U.S. 424 (1976), 434.

18. Charles L. Glenn, Kahris McLaughlin, and Laura Salganik, *Parent Information for School Choice: The Case of Massachusetts* (Boston: Center of Families, Communities, Schools, and Children's Learning, Institute for Responsive Education, 1993), p. 1. Clinchy and Kolb, *Planning for School Choice*, pp. 4–5.

19. See, for example, Snider, "The Call for Choice," p. C1; Rossell, "The Buffalo Controlled Choice Plan," p. 332; Steel and Levine, *Educational Innovation in Multiracial Contexts*, p. ii. Dana Milbank, "Schoolyard Tussle," *New Republic*, December 14, 1998, pp. 22, 23.

20. John Ritter, "New Con: Sneaking into School, Parents Lie to Better

Kids' Education," *USA Today*, January 22, 1997, p. 1A. Orfield, *City-Suburban Desegregation*, pp. 2, 14. Orfield, *Must We Bus?* p. 414; Orfield and Eaton, *Dismantling Desegregation*, p. 311.

21. Judith Havemann, "Benefactors Create Their Own School Voucher Programs," *Washington Post*, February 21, 1998, p. A1. Rene Sanchez, "Cleveland Charts New Educational Course," *Washington Post*, September 10, 1996, p. A1. Terry Moe, "The Public Revolution Private Money Might Bring," *Washington Post*, May 9, 1999, p. B3; Jeff Archer, "Huge Demand for Private Vouchers Raises Questions," *Education Week*, April 28, 1999.

22. Steve Farkas and Jean Johnson, *Time to Move On: African-American and White Parents Set an Agenda for Public Schools: A Report from Public Agenda* (New York: Public Agenda, 1998), p. 18; see also Fleigel, *Miracle in East Harlem*, p. 195. Kathleen Sylvester, "Common Standards, Diverse Schools: Renewing the Promise of Public Education," in Will Marshall, ed., *Building the Bridge* (Lanham, Md.: Rowman and Littlefield, 1997), pp. 75–76.

23. Alves, "Comments and General Discussion," in Rasell and Rothstein, *School Choice*, p. 143; see also Rossell and Glenn, "The Cambridge Controlled Choice Plan," p. 85; Christine H. Rossell, "Controlled-Choice Desegregation Plans: Not Enough Choice, Too Much Control?" *Urban Affairs Review*, vol. 31 (September 1995), p. 73. Bob Gittens, interview by author, December 2, 1997, Boston, p. 10.

24. Alves, "Comments and General Discussion," in Rasell and Rothstein, *School Choice*, p. 143; see also Rossell and Glenn, "The Cambridge Controlled Choice Plan," p. 85; Rossell, "Not Enough Choice, Too Much Control?" pp. 31, 73. Gittens, interview, p. 10. Clewell and Joy, *Choice in Montclair*, p. 6. Kirkpatrick, *Choice in Schooling*, p. 74.

25. See Fuller and Elmore, *Who Chooses? Who Loses?* p. 192; Christine H. Rossell, *The Carrot or the Stick for School Desegregation Policy: Magnet Schools or Forced Busing* (Temple University Press, 1990), p. 116; Edward B. Fiske and Helen F. Ladd, *When Schools Compete: A Cautionary Tale* (Brookings, 2000), p. 196.

26. Richard F. Elmore, "Choice as an Instrument of Public Policy: Evidence from Education and Health Care," in William H. Clune and John F. Witte, eds., *Choice and Control in American Education*, vol. 1, *The Theory of Choice and Control in Education* (London: Falmer Press, 1990), p. 308. Alves and Willie, "Controlled Choice—An Approach to Effective School Desegregation," p. 84; see also Rossell and Glenn, "The Cambridge Controlled Choice Plan," pp. 85–86. Michael Alves, "Comments and General Discussion," in Rasell and Rothstein, *School Choice*, p. 137; Rothstein, "Introduction," in Rasell and Rothstein, *School Choice*, p. 22; Glenn, "Controlled Choice in Massachusetts Public Schools," p. 97. Charles Glenn, interview by author, December 3, 1997, Boston, pp. 15, 17.

27. Wilkinson, *From* Brown *to* Bakke, p. 142. Edward Banfield, *Unheavenly Cities* (Boston: Little, Brown, 1968), p. 79 (on 1964 data); Bok, *The State of the*

Nation, pp. 178–79 (on today's desire for integration). Wilson, *When Work Disappears*, pp. 10–11. Douglas S. Massey and Nancy A. Denton, *American Apartheid: Segregation and the Making of the Underclass* (Harvard University Press, 1993), pp. 89–90, cited in John A. Powell, "Living and Learning: Linking Housing and Education," *Minnesota Law Review*, vol. 80 (April 1996), p. 786 n. 125. Valerie E. Lee, Robert G. Croninger, and Julia B. Smith, "Equity and Choice in Detroit," in Fuller and Elmore, *Who Chooses? Who Loses?* p. 83. Abigail Thernstrom and Stephan Thernstrom, "Black Progress: How Far We've Come and How Far We Have to Go," *Brookings Review* (spring 1998), p. 12; see also Edith McArthur and others, *Use of School Choice, Educational Policy Issues: Statistical Perspectives* (NCES, 1995), p. 2.

28. See Clewall and Joy, *Choice in Montclair*, pp. 7, 10, 17.

29. Rossell and Glenn, "The Cambridge Controlled Choice Plan," p. 81.

30. Tan, *The Cambridge Controlled Choice Program*, p. 11; Peter W. Cookson Jr., *School Choice: The Struggle for the Soul of America* (Yale University Press, 1994) pp. 61, 63; Young and Clinchy, *Choice in Public Education*, pp. 28–29, 61–65, 80, 83–84, 105–06; Helen Machado, "Group to Fight School Choice in Manchester," *Hartford Courant*, February 28, 1996, p. B1; Laura Ungar, "Controlled Choice Greeted with Dissent," p. B1; Hicks, "Some Families Find the Choice Limited," p. A1; Henig, *Rethinking School Choice*, pp. 123–24; Chrissie Bamber and others, *Public School Choice: An Equal Chance for All?* (Columbia, Md.: National Committee for Citizens in Education, 1990), p. 25; Clewell and Joy, *Choice in Montclair*, pp. 6–10. These high figures do not reflect "gaming" by parents; see Glenn, McLaughlin, and Salganik, *Parent Information for School Choice*, p. 14; and Glenn, *Family Choice and Public Schools: A Report to the State Board of Education*, p. 27.

31. Glenn, *Family Choice and Public Schools*, p. 29; see also Glenn, McLaughlin, and Salganik, *Parent Information for School Choice*, p. 16; Glenn, "Controlled Choice in Massachusetts Public Schools," pp. 98–99. Torres, "Controlled Choice?" p. A1. Boston subsequently eliminated controlled choice, not from a popular uprising but because of a lawsuit; see chapter 8.

32. For critics, see, for example, Thernstrom and Thernstrom, "Black Progress," p. 319; Fierman, "Giving Parents a Choice of Schools," p. 147. McArthur and others, *Use of School Choice*, p. 1; Susan Choy, *Public and Private Schools: How They Differ* (NCES, 1997), pp. 3–4.

33. Choy, *Public and Private Schools*, pp. 5, 3–4; Elmore, "Choice as an Instrument of Public Policy," pp. 300–01. McArthur and others, *Use of School Choice*, p. 1.

34. Jeffrey R. Henig and Stephen D. Sugarman, "The Nature and Extent of School Choice," in Stephen D. Sugarman and Frank R. Kemerer, eds., *School Choice and Social Controversy* (Brookings, 1999), pp. 29 (36 percent), 16 (wealthier more likely). Michael Alves, interview by author, December 1, 1997, Cambridge, p. 43. Charles L. Glenn, "Free Schools and the Revival of

Urban Communities," paper prepared for *Welfare Responsibility: An Inquiry into the Roots of America's Welfare Crisis*, a project of the Center for Public Justice, funded by the Pew Charitable Trusts, October 1993, p. 9.

35. Glenn, McLaughlin, and Salganik, *Parent Information for School Choice*, p. 18.

36. See Anthony Giddens, *The Third Way: The Renewal of Social Democracy* (Oxford: Blackwell, 1998), p. 65.

37. Wells, *Time to Choose*, p. 5 (paraphrasing Joe Nathan).

38. See, for example, Patrick Welsh, "It's No Longer Uncool to Do Well in School," *Washington Post*, March 14, 1999, p. B2.

39. Fiske and Ladd, *When Schools Compete*, pp. 184–95, 197–98.

40. *Missouri v. Jenkins II*, 115 S.Ct. 2038 (1995) 2042 (that with lavish expenditure, system remains 68 percent black); 2054 (that per pupil noncapital costs were much higher); James S. Kunen, "The End of Integration," *Time*, April 29, 1996, pp. 41–42; Dennis Farney, "Integration Is Faltering in Kansas City Schools as Priorities Change," *Wall Street Journal*, September 26, 1995, p. A1; Stephan Thernstrom and Abigail Thernstrom, *America in Black and White* (Simon and Schuster, 1997), pp. 345–46; see also Lisa Frazier, "Prince George's Schools Struggle with Racial Plan," *Washington Post*, April 2, 1996, p. C1; Orfield, *Must We Bus?* p. 405; Young and Clinchy, *Choice in Public Education*, pp. 23–24. Myron Orfield, *Metropolitics: A Regional Agenda for Community and Stability* (Brookings, 1997), p. 45.

41. Christopher Jencks, "Is the Public School Obsolete?" *Public Interest*, vol. 2 (winter 1966), pp. 25–26; see also Charles Glenn, "Putting School Choice in Place," *Phi Delta Kappan*, vol. 71 (December 1989), p. 295. "A Scholar Who Inspired It Says Busing Backfired," interview with James Coleman, *National Observer*, June 7, 1975, p. 18; Robin M. Bennefield, "Cette ecole est publique," *U.S. News and World Report*, October 7, 1996, pp. 62–63.

42. See, for example, Henig, *Rethinking School Choice*, pp. 165–66; Jeffrey Henig, "Choice in Public Schools: An Analysis of Transfer Requests among Magnet Schools," *Social Science Quarterly*, vol. 71 (March 1990), pp. 69, 76; Bruce Fuller, Richard F. Elmore, and Gary Orfield, "Policymaking in the Dark: Illuminating the School Choice Debate," in Fuller and Elmore, *Who Chooses? Who Loses?* pp. 13–14; Lee, Croninger, and Smith, "Equity and Choice in Detroit," p. 71; Richard F. Elmore and Bruce Fuller, "Empirical Research on Educational Choice: What Are the Implications for Policymaking?" in Fuller and Elmore, *Who Chooses? Who Loses?* p. 189; Isabel Wilkerson, "Des Moines Acts to Halt White Flight after State Allows Choice of Schools," *New York Times*, December 16, 1992, p. B9; Amy Stuart Wells, "Quest for Improving Schools Finds Role for Free Market," *New York Times*, March 14, 1990, p. A1.

43. Valerie Martinez, Kenneth Godwin, and Frank R. Kemerer, "Public School Choice in San Antonio: Who Chooses and with What Effects?" in Fuller and Elmore, *Who Chooses? Who Loses?* pp. 51, 57–58; Rothstein, introduction to Rasell

and Rothstein, *School Choice*, pp. 6–9, 12; Witte, "Who Benefits from the Milwaukee Choice Program?" pp. 123–25; Carol Ascher and Gary Burnett, *Current Trends and Issues in Urban Education, 1993* (New York: ERIC Clearinghouse on Urban Education, 1993), p. 22; Fiske and Ladd, *When Schools Compete*, p. 206. Glenn, "Putting School Choice in Place," p. 297. Richard Elmore and Bruce Fuller, "Empirical Research on Education Choice: What Are the Implications for Policy-Making?" in Fuller and Elmore, *Who Chooses? Who Loses?* p. 192.

44. Alves and Willie, "Controlled Choice," p. 79. See also Meier, *The Power of Their Ideas*, p. 94. Thomas Toch, *Improving Performance*, p. 8. Education Commission of the States, *A State Policy-Makers' Guide*, p. 34. Some object to the notion that all parents will choose schools—Abigail Thernstrom worries about "drugged parents who won't and probably can't make informed choices"—but that is all the more reason to create a mechanism under which middle-class families will be in all schools, thereby creating pressure for all schools to improve; Glenn, "Controlled Choice in Massachusetts Public Schools," p. 97.

45. Richard D. Kahlenberg, *The Remedy: Class, Race, and Affirmative Action* (New York: Basic Books, 1996), pp. 148–51 (arguing for a class-based preference in admissions to selective high schools, because counting obstacles is relevant in meritocratic determinations about young people, but not arguing for proportional representation).

46. Gary Natriello, Edward L. McDill, and Aaron M. Pallas, *Schooling Disadvantaged Children: Racing against Catastrophe* (New York: Teachers College Press, 1990), p.185. Glenn, *Family Choice of Schools*, p. 38.

47. Barbara Chriss, Greta Nash, and David Stern, "The Rise and Fall of Choice in Richmond, California," *Economics of Education Review*, vol. 11 (December 1992), p. 395; William Snider, "California District Makes Choice Initiative Centerpiece of Plan to Reinvigorate Schools," *Education Week*, December 13, 1989, p. 22. Myron Lieberman, *Public School Choice: Current Issues, Future Prospects* (Lancaster, Pa.: Technomic Publishing, 1990), pp. 35–37, 38–40, 62–63; John McAdams, "Can Open Enrollment Work?" *Public Interest*, vol. 37 (fall 1974), pp. 72–77, 83–84; see also Amy Stuart Wells and others, *Beyond the Rhetoric of Charter School Reform: A Study of Ten California School Districts* (Los Angeles: UCLA Charter School Study, 1998), p. 48. Steel and Levine, *Educational Innovation in Multiracial Contexts*, p.101.

48. Wilkinson, *From* Brown *to* Bakke, pp. 113–14. Fliegel, *Miracle in East Harlem*, p.187.

49. Snider, "The Call for Choice," p. C8; Ascher and Burnett, *Current Trends and Issues in Urban Education*, p. 20; Rossell, *The Carrot or the Stick*, p. 200; Jennifer L. Hochschild, *The New American Dilemma: Liberal Democracy and School Desegregation* (Yale University Press, 1984), p. 76. Lemann, "Magnetic Attraction," p. 17. Farkas and Johnson, *Time to Move On*, pp. 28–29.

50. Ascher and Burnett, *Current Trends and Issues in Urban Education*, p. 19. William L. Yancey and Salvatore J. Saporito, *Racial and Economic Segregation and*

Educational Outcomes: One Tale, Two Cities (Philadelphia: Temple University Center for Research in Human Development and Education, 1995), pp. 18, 26–27. Carmel McCoubrey, "Magnet Schools and Class," *New York Times*, June 23, 1999, p. A18. Department of Education, "Education Innovation in Multiracial Contexts, Highlights," 1994 (www.ed.gov/offices/OUS/eval/esed/magnet2.html [March 2, 1999]) (summarizing Steel and Levine, *Education Innovation in Multiracial Contexts*). Lemann, "Magnetic Attraction," p. 17.

51. Donald R. Moore and Suzanne Davenport, "High School Choice and Students at Risk," *Equity and Choice*, vol. 5 (February 1989), pp. 5–6; Glenn, "Controlled Choice in Massachusetts Public Schools," pp. 93–94. Ascher and Burnett, *Current Trends and Issues in Urban Education*, p. 19. Nathan, "Charters and Choice," p. 74. Ron Suskind, *A Hope in the Unseen: An American Odyssey from the Inner City to the Ivy League* (New York: Broadway, 1998), p. 37. David Nakamura, "School 'Contract' Draws Complaints," *Washington Post*, April 16, 1999, p. B1. William Snider, "School Choice: New, More Efficient 'Sorting Machine'?" *Education Week*, May 18, 1988, p. 8. William Snider, "Parley on 'Choice,' Final Budget Mark Transition," *Education Week*, January 18, 1989, p. 24. Hochschild, *The New American Dilemma*, p. 77.

52. Wells, *Time to Choose*, p. 86.

53. Young and Clinchy, *Choice in Public Education*, pp. 23–24. Hochschild, *The New American Dilemma*, p. 72. Rolf Blank, "Educational Effects of Magnet High Schools," in Clune and Witte, *Choice and Control in American Education*, vol. 2, *The Practice of Choice*, p. 77.

54. Clewall and Joy, *Choice in Montclair*, pp. 5–6. Glenn, "Controlled Choice in Massachusetts Public Schools," p. 95.

55. See Glenn, McLaughlin, and Salganik, *Parent Information for School Choice*, p. 8.

Eliminating Poverty Concentrations through Public School Choice

1. See, e.g., David C. Berliner, "Averages that Hide the True Extremes," *Washington Post*, January 28, 2001, p. B3.

2. National Center for Education Statistics, *NEAP 1998 Reading Report Card for the Nation* (Washington, D.C.: U.S. Department of Education, 1999), pp. 44, 59.

3. David J. Hoff, "World-Class Education Eludes Many in the U.S.," *Education Week*, April 11, 2001, pp. 1, 14–15.

4. Samuel Casey Carter, *No Excuses: Lessons from 21 High-Performing High-Poverty Schools* (Washington, D.C.: Heritage Foundation, 2000). Maria Newman, "Federal Law on Failing Schools Has States Scrambling to Comply,"

New York Times, July 4, 2002, p. B1 (on 8,600 low-performing schools). More recently, the Education Trust released a study purportedly identifying 4,577 high-poverty or high-minority schools that achieve at high levels. See Craig D. Jerald, *Dispelling the Myth Revisited: Preliminary Findings from a Nationwide Analysis of "High-Flying" Schools* (Washington, D.C: The Education Trust, 2001). Further analysis of the study's data, however, found that when a more meaningful definition of "high achievement" was applied, only one-half of 1 percent of high-poverty and high-minority schools had high scores in reading and math in two grades for two years running. See Richard Rothstein, "An Accountability Push and Fuzzy Math," *New York Times*, April 10, 2002, p. A21.

5. *Education Week*, in collaboration with the Pew Charitable Trusts, sought to identify a "solidly successful urban district, in which even extremely poor and minority children achieve at high levels," but concluded that "there are none." See "Quality Counts '98: The Urban Challenge," *Education Week*, January 8, 1998, p. 6.

6. Mary M. Kennedy, Richard K. Jung, and M. E. Orland, *Poverty, Achievement, and the Distribution of Compensatory Education Services: An Interim Report from the National Assessment of Chapter 1* (Washington, D.C.: U.S. Department of Education, 1986), pp. 21–22. This particular study cites raw scores rather than growth in scores over time, which may reflect in some measure self-selection bias (low-income families who are determined to live in middle-class school districts may be particularly motivated). But most studies attempt to control for this and find that when measuring growth in achievement over time—the "value added" by the school—high-poverty schools continue to rank below middle-class schools. See, e.g., Jay Mathews, "Testing Students, Scoring Teachers: Tennessee System for Gauging Results Angers Some Educators but Gains Acceptance Elsewhere," *Washington Post*, March 14, 2000, p. A7.

7. James S. Coleman et al., *Equality of Educational Opportunity* (Washington, D.C.: Government Printing Office, 1966), p. 22. For a recent summary of studies over the last forty years, see Richard D. Kahlenberg, *All Together Now: Creating Middle Class Schools through Public School Choice* (Washington, D.C.: Brookings Institution Press, 2001), pp. 25–37.

8. Stephanie Stullich, Brenda Donly, and Simeon Stolzberg, *Targeting Schools: Study of Title I Allocations Within School Districts* (Washington, D.C.: U.S. Department of Education, 1999).

9. Gary Orfield and Susan Eaton, *Dismantling Desegregation: The Quiet Reversal of* Brown v. Board of Education (New York: New Press, 1996), p. 53.

10. While one in twenty poor whites live in neighborhoods with more than 40 percent of residents living in poverty, one in three poor blacks do. David Rusk, *Inside Game/Outside Game: Winning Strategies for Saving Urban America* (Washington, D.C: Brookings Institution Press, 1999), p. 72.

11. See, e.g., Esther Ho Sui-Chu and J. Douglas Willms, "Effects of Parental Involvement on Eighth-Grade Achievement," *Sociology of Education* 69 (April 1996): 130, 135, 138 (in math and reading "the SES of a school had an effect on achievement that was comparable to the effects associated with the SES of a family"); Stephen Schellenberg, "Concentration of Poverty and Ongoing Need for Title I," in Gary Orfield and Elizabeth DeBray, eds., *Hard Work for Good Schools: Facts Not Fads in Title I Reform* (Cambridge, Mass.: Harvard Civil Rights Project, 1999), p. 130 ("the degree to which poor children are surrounded by other poor children, both in their neighborhood and at school, has as strong an effect on their achievement as their own poverty").

12. Robert Crain study of state achievement gaps by segregation, cited in Megan Twohey, "Desegregation Is Dead," *National Journal*, September 18, 1999, p. 2619. For a more recent confirmation of Crain's studies on the relationship between racial segregation and student achievement, see Roslyn Arlin Mickelson, "Subverting Swann: First and Second Generation Segregation in Charlotte-Mecklenburg Schools," *American Educational Research Journal* 38, no. 2 (summer 2001): 215–52 (attending a racially isolated elementary school has a negative effect on black achievement).

13. Jonathan Guryan, "Desegregation and Black Dropout Rates," NBER Working Paper 8345, National Bureau of Economic Research, Cambridge, Mass., June 2001.

14. Claude S. Fischer et al., *Inequality by Design: Cracking the Bell Curve Myth* (Princeton, N.J.: Princeton University Press, 1996), pp. 83–84.

15. See, e.g., William J. Fowler Jr., ed., *Developments in School Finance* (Washington, D.C.: U.S. Department of Education, 1995).

16. Paul Barton and Richard Coley, *America's Smallest School: The Family* (Princeton, N.J.: Educational Testing Service, 1992), p. 37.

17. See Michael J. Puma et al., *Prospects: Final Report on Student Outcomes* (Cambridge, Mass.: Abt Associates, 1997), p. v.

18. Betty Hart and Todd R. Risley, *Meaningful Differences in the Everyday Experience of Young American Children* (Baltimore, Md.: Paul H. Brookes Publishing Co., 1995).

19. See, e.g., Beatrice Birman et al., *The Current Operation of the Chapter 1 Program* (Washington, D.C.: U.S. Department of Education, 1987), pp. 92–93; Puma et al., *Prospects*, p. B3.

20. National Center for Education Statistics, *Teacher Quality: A Report on the Preparation and Qualifications of Public School Teachers* (Washington, D.C.: U.S. Department of Education, 1999), p. 17 (teaching out of field); John F. Kain and Kraig Singleton, "Equality of Educational Opportunity Revisited," *New England Economic Review*, May–June 1996, pp. 87, 99, 107 (teacher test scores); and Laura Lipmann and others, *Urban Schools: The Challenge of Location and Poverty* (Washington, D.C.: National Center for Education Statistics, 1996), pp. 86–88, 96 (experience). Minority students are also less likely to have experienced

teachers according to new research in North Carolina conducted by Helen F. Ladd and colleagues. See Debra Viadero, "Study: Teachers Seek Better Working Conditions," *Education Week*, January 9, 2002, p. 5.

21. For a summary of studies, see Kati Haycock, "Good Teaching Matters," *Thinking K–16* 3, no. 2 (summer 1998): 3–13.

22. See, e.g., Gary Orfield and Susan Eaton, *Dismantling Desegregation*, pp. 25, 83; Michael J. Puma et al., *Prospects*, pp. vi, 12. Experience abroad is also sobering. The Dutch system, for example, provides nearly twice as much money for low-income students, and has not produced positive results. See David Rusk, Dirk Frieling, and Leon Groenemejjer, *Inside Game/Outside Game: Segregation and Spatial Planning in Metropolitan Areas* (Amsterdam and Delft: ABF Stragie, March 2001), pp. 72–82.

23. Eric A. Hanushek, John F. Kain, and Steven G. Rivkin, "Why Public Schools Lose Teachers," NBER Working Paper No. W8599, National Bureau of Economic Research, Cambridge, Mass., November 2001. See also Viadero, "Study," p. 5.

24. See, e.g., Randy Ross, "How Class-Size Reduction Harms Kids in Poor Neighborhoods," *Education Week*, May 26, 1999, p. 30.

25. See, e.g., Birman, *The Current Operation of Chapter 1*, pp. 94–95; Eric Brunner and Jon Sonstelie, "Coping with Serrano: Voluntary Contributions to California's Local Public Schools," paper presented to the National Tax Association's Eighty-Ninth Annual Conference on Taxation, Boston, November 10–12, 1996, pp. 372–81.

26. *McCollum v. Board of Education*, 333 U.S. 203 (1948), 216 and 231 (Frankfurter, J., concurring).

27. See, e.g., Amy Stuart Wells and Robert L. Crain, "Perpetuation Theory and the Long-Term Effects of School Desegregation," *Review of Educational Research* 64, no. 4 (1994): 531–55; Charles V. Willie and Jerome Baker, *Race Mixing in Public Schools* (New York: Praeger, 1973), p. 3; Jomills Henry Braddock II, Robert L. Crain, and James M. McPartland, "A Long-Term View of School Desegregation: Some Recent Studies of Graduates as Adults," *Phi Delta Kappan* 66, no. 4 (December 1984): 260; Nancy A. Denton, "The Persistence of Segregation," *Minnesota Law Review* 80 (April 1996): 822–23.

28. See National Center for Education Statistics, *Digest of Education Statistics, 1999* (Washington, D.C.: U.S. Government Printing Office, 2000), table 379 (33.2 percent of students receive federally subsidized lunches). J. Anderson, *The Distribution of Chapter 1 Services* (Washington, D.C: U.S. Department of Education, 1993) (one-quarter of schools majority low income). The data in Duncan Chaplin's background paper for this Task Force show a 45 percent subsidized lunch participation rate among districts reporting data (Table B.1). This number may be higher because of missing data (Chaplin estimates, based on census data, that the true eligibility rate is 36 percent) and because his data involve only elementary schools, where FARM data tend

to be higher because parents are younger and less economically secure as a group than older parents.

29. Gary Orfield with Nora Gordon, *Schools More Separate: Consequences of a Decade of Resegregation* (Cambridge, Mass.: Harvard Civil Rights Project, July 2001), Table 9.

30. Id.

31. See *Board of Education of Oklahoma City v. Dowell*, 498 U.S. 237 (1991); *Freeman v. Pitts*, 503 U.S. 467 (1992); and *Missouri v. Jencks*, 115 S.Ct. 2038 (1995).

32. This is an emerging theme from the ongoing Understanding Race and Education Study by UCLA–Teachers College for which Amy Stuart Wells is the principal investigator.

33. William Julius Wilson, *When Work Disappears: The World of the New Urban Poor* (New York: Knopf, 1996), p. 149.

34. See, e.g., Jeffrey Henig, *Rethinking School Choice: Limits of the Marketplace Metaphor* (Princeton, N.J.: Princeton University Press, 1994), pp. 165–66; Bruce Fuller and Richard Elmore, eds., *Who Chooses? Who Loses? Culture, Institutions and the Unequal Effects of School Choice* (New York: Teachers College Press, 1996), pp. 13–14, 189; Edward B. Fiske and Helen F. Ladd, *When Schools Compete: A Cautionary Tale* (Washington, D.C.: Brookings Institution Press, 2000).

35. See Charles Willie and Michael Alves, *Controlled Choice: A New Approach to School Desegregated Education and School Improvement*, Education Alliance Press and the New England Desegregation Assistance Center, Brown University, Providence, R.I., 1996.

36. See, e.g., Peter W. Cookson Jr., *School Choice: The Struggle for the Soul of America* (New Haven, Conn.: Yale University Press, 1994), pp. 61, 63; Henig, *Rethinking School Choice*, pp. 123–24.

37. For example, in Seattle, Washington, when poor children received 36 percent more funding than other students, middle-class schools did not treat this amount of money as sufficient incentive to recruit low-income children. See Kim Murphy, "Seattle's School Program Sets Off Marketing Frenzy," *Los Angeles Times*, April 9, 1998, p. A1. One recent study suggested that the cost of providing an adequate education to low-income children is more than double (139 percent more) than the cost of educating other children. See *Report of the Commission on Education Finance, Equity, and Excellence* (Thornton Commission), State of Maryland, November 9, 2001, p. 3.

38. "Backing the Bus," *New Republic*, February 24, 1982, p. 7; Gary Orfield, *Must We Bus? Segregated Schools and National Policy* (Washington, D.C.: Brookings Institution Press, 1978), p. 114.

39. *Digest of Education Statistics 2000* (Washington, D.C.: U.S. Department of Education, 2001), Table 52. Even under St. Louis's plan, which involved

interdistrict choice (longer distances), and, originally, allowed choice of any of 122 schools within sixteen suburban areas (as opposed to more limited choice within a given geographic zone), the cost per pupil was $2000, which the business community believed to be a far better investment than compensatory spending in segregated schools. See the background paper by William Freivogel for this Task Force.

40. "Active Community Environments," U.S. Department of Health and Human Services, Washington, D.C., May 2000.

41. Terry Moe, *Schools, Vouchers, and the American Public* (Washington, D.C.: Brookings Institution Press, 2001), p. 333.

42. Steve Farkas and Jean Johnson, *Time to Move On: African-American and White Parents Set an Agenda for Public Schools* (New York: Public Agenda, 1998), p. 41.

43. Lynn Schnaiberg, "More Students Taking Advantage of School Choice, Report Says," *Education Week*, September 22, 1999, p. 6 (citing report by Policy Analysis for California Education that 6.7 million students attend public schools of choice compared with 5.2 million attending private schools).

44. David Rusk, "The 'Segregation Tax,'" Brookings Institution Center on Urban and Metropolitan Policy Survey Series, Washington, D.C., October 2001, p. 9.

45. Sandra Feldman, Statement to the Task Force, June 5, 2001.

46. Jodi Wilgoren, "Chicago Uses Preschool to Lure Middle Class," *New York Times*, June 15, 2001, p. A1.

47. Carole Bass, "The Iron Sheff," *Fairfield County Weekly*, September 27, 2001, p. 10.

48. See William H. Frey, "Melting Pot Suburbs: A Census 2000 Study of Suburban Diversity," Brookings Center on Urban and Metropolitan Policy Census 2000 Series, Washington, D.C., June 2001. See also D'Vera Cohn and Sarah Cohen, "D.C. Region a Growth Capital," *Washington Post*, April 3, 2001, p. A1. (In Washington, D.C., metropolitan area, 74.8 percent of blacks live in the suburbs. In Atlanta, the figure is 78.5 percent. By contrast, in New York City, the figure is 6.8 percent.)

49. "Quality Counts," *Education Week*, January 8, 1998, p. 9.

50. Orfield with Gordon, *Schools More Separate*, p.1.

51. Jeffrey R. Henig and Stephen D. Sugarman, "The Nature and Extent of School Choice," in Stephen D. Sugarman and Frank R. Kemerer, eds., *School Choice and Social Controversy* (Washington, D.C.: Brookings Institution Press, 1999), p. 29 (300,000 use interdistrict public school choice); Diane Ravitch, "The Right Thing: Why Liberals Should Be Pro-Choice," *New Republic*, October 8, 2001, p. 35 (14,000 publicly funded voucher students).

52. See, e.g., Bruce Katz and Joel Rogers, "Metropolitan Power," in Robert L. Borosage and Roger Hickey, eds., *The Next Agenda* (Boulder, Colo.: Westview Press, 2001), p. 195 (every $1,000 gained or lost in per capita city

income associated with at least a $690 gain or loss in per capita suburban income).

53. The consensus on this point ranges from Diane Ravitch, *The Troubled Crusade: American Education 1945–1980* (New York: Basic Books, 1983), p. 167, to Gary Orfield, *Must We Bus?*, p. 279.

54. David Rusk, October 31, 2001, Task Force meeting.

55. The leading articles on this topic are James E. Ryan, "*Sheff*, Segregation, and School Finance Litigation," *New York University Law Review* 74 (May 1999): 529–573; and James E. Ryan, "Schools, Race, and Money," *Yale Law Journal* 109 (November 1999): 249–316.

56. Although the court in *Sheff* relied on a combination of constitutional provisions, saying that the right to an equal education is "informed" by a fairly unusual constitutional provision against segregation—the basic reasoning in *Sheff* could be applied in states that lack Connecticut's segregation clause. See Ryan, "*Sheff*," p. 546. The Minneapolis case was settled out of court, and the Rochester plaintiffs are appealing a negative decision, but advocates recall that *Brown* itself took many years of hard work to win, and then to enforce.